SpringerBriefs in Business

SpringerBriefs present concise summaries of cutting-edge research and practical applications across a wide spectrum of fields. Featuring compact volumes of 50 to 125 pages, the series covers a range of content from professional to academic. Typical topics might include:

- A timely report of state-of-the art analytical techniques
- A bridge between new research results, as published in journal articles, and a contextual literature review
- A snapshot of a hot or emerging topic
- An in-depth case study or clinical example
- A presentation of core concepts that students must understand in order to make independent contributions

SpringerBriefs in Business showcase emerging theory, empirical research, and practical application in management, finance, entrepreneurship, marketing, operations research, and related fields, from a global author community.

Briefs are characterized by fast, global electronic dissemination, standard publishing contracts, standardized manuscript preparation and formatting guidelines, and expedited production schedules.

Paul Chiambaretto • Emmanuel Combe

Introduction to Air Transport

Economics, Business Models, and Future Challenges

Springer

Paul Chiambaretto
MBS School of Business
Montpellier, France

Emmanuel Combe
University of Paris 1 Panthéon-Sorbonne
Paris, France

ISSN 2191-5482 ISSN 2191-5490 (electronic)
SpringerBriefs in Business
ISBN 978-3-031-99935-2 ISBN 978-3-031-99936-9 (eBook)
https://doi.org/10.1007/978-3-031-99936-9

Originally published by La Découverte, France, 2023

Translation from the French language edition: "Le transport aérien" by Paul Chiambaretto and Emmanuel Combe, © La Découverte 2023. Published by La Découverte. All Rights Reserved.

This Springer imprint is published by the registered company Springer Nature Switzerland AG
The registered company address is: Gewerbestrasse 11, 6330 Cham, Switzerland

Introduction

With more than 5 billion passengers expected in 2025, commercial aviation is now a widespread means of transport in both developed and emerging countries. Its rise is relatively recent, driven by several revolutions since its beginnings 120 years ago: a technological revolution with the launch of the jet engine in the 1950s; a regulatory revolution with the opening up of competition since the 1980s; a commercial revolution with the rise of low-cost airlines in the 1990s; and a geopolitical revolution with the rise of new hubs, notably in the Middle East, since the 2000s.

This book offers an overview of the functioning, developments, and challenges facing the air transport industry, using a triple approach: economic, systemic, and prospective. The economic approach helps understand how an airline operates, by identifying the different sources of costs and revenues, depending on the type of airline and the flight distance. The systemic analysis takes into account the context and ecosystem in which airlines operate. The prospective dimension aims to set out the main challenges that air transport will have to face in the future, foremost among which is climate change.

In Chap. 1, we present the major milestones in air transport and the main factors driving its development. This analysis is useful for forecasting future traffic growth.

Chapter 2 discusses the various players in the air transport ecosystem: aircraft and engine manufacturers, aircraft lessors, ticket reservation systems, and airports. In addition, we show that passenger air transport is heavily regulated not only by sector-specific rules that affect many areas, including flight safety and slot access at major airports, but also by general rules, such as competition law.

In Chap. 3, we focus on airlines' business model, presenting the various fixed and variable costs, before analyzing their revenues. In particular, we discuss the key role of dynamic pricing, where the price of a ticket on the same flight evolves over time.

In Chap. 4, we analyze the competitive interactions between airlines. In the short- and medium-haul market, we show that the low-cost revolution has profoundly reshuffled the deck, with the success of cost domination strategies. We also show that in the long-haul market, competition between airlines takes a less direct form, notably through differentiation strategies and efforts to move upmarket, even though some players are attempting to apply low-cost recipes.

Chapter 5, which looks toward the future, addresses three challenges facing the air transport industry. The first challenge is climate change, at a time when the European Union and many other countries are moving toward carbon neutrality. We show that the solutions implemented in the air transport sector are not only technological but also regulatory and fiscal. The second challenge is changing customer behavior. In the case of business travel, the challenge is to determine whether the rise of videoconferencing will have a lasting impact on traffic growth. The third challenge is a country's air transport sovereignty. We show that this presupposes technological capabilities in aircraft manufacturing, as Russia and China are attempting to master today.

With more than 5 billion passengers expected in 2025, commercial aviation is today a widely used means of transportation around the world. This book offers an overview of the functioning, evolution, and challenges faced by this sector, focusing on a triple approach: economic, systemic, and prospective. The economic approach enables a better understanding of how an airline operates by identifying its sources of costs and revenues according to the type of airline and the flight distance. The systemic analysis invites consideration of the context and ecosystem in which airline activities are embedded: aircraft manufacturers, airports, regulators. The prospective dimension aims to directly address the main challenges that air transportation will have to face in the future, such as climate change and the quest for economic sovereignty.

Contents

About the Authors

Paul Chiambaretto is full professor of strategic management at MBS School of Business and an associate researcher at École Polytechnique. As a specialist in air transport economics and management, he is the director of the Chaire Pégase, a research institute dedicated to these subjects. He is a graduate of the Ecole Normale Supérieure and holds a PhD in management science from the École Polytechnique. He has written many research articles on the strategies of air transport players (e.g., airlines, airports, manufacturers).

Emmanuel Combe is full professor of economics at the University of Paris 1 Panthéon-Sorbonne and affiliated professor at Skema Business School. He is a graduate of the Ecole Normale Supérieure and holds a PhD in economics from the University of Paris 1 Panthéon-Sorbonne. He was Vice-Chairman of the French Competition Authority from 2012 to 2022. He is the author of "Le low cost" (2nd edition, 2019) and "La politique de la concurrence" (3rd edition, 2016).

Chapter 1
The Evolution of Air Transport and Its Impact

In this chapter, we present the major stages in the evolution of air transport, highlighting both its determinants and its economic impact. In the first part, we identify the five major stages that have shaped the evolution of air transport since the Wright brothers' first flight in 1903, with a particular emphasis on the period of liberalization that began in 1978. In the second part, we discuss the structural causes that determine the evolution of traffic: mainly the economic growth rate and the evolution of airfares. Finally, the third section details the local and global impact of transport on economic growth and employment.

1.1 Milestones in the Air Transport History

1.1.1 1903–1944: The Time of the Pioneers

While the French often consider Clément Ader the first person to have flown an engine-powered machine (in 1890), history records the American brothers Orville and Wilbur Wright as the true pioneers of aviation, with their first flight on December 17, 1903.[1] The achievements of the Wright brothers generated considerable enthusiasm both throughout Europe and in the United States, inspiring the first generation of pilots. These first pilots, who were often also the designers of their own aircrafts, set out to break altitude, speed, and time records. Likewise, new materials were tested: whereas the first planes were made of wood, cloth, or paper, metal planes appeared during World War I, marking the start of military use of aircraft.

[1] The reason for this choice is that, unlike Clément Ader, the Wright brothers were able to repeat the feat of flying, on several occasions and in public, showing that they had truly mastered their flights. Clément Ader will go down in history for having invented the word "avion" ("airplane" in French).

P. Chiambaretto, E. Combe, *Introduction to Air Transport*, SpringerBriefs in Business, https://doi.org/10.1007/978-3-031-99936-9_1

Technological improvements led to longer flights, enabling the first aviators to cross the English Channel (Louis Blériot in 1909), the Mediterranean Sea (Roland Garros in 1913), and the Atlantic Ocean (Charles Lindbergh in 1927).

These improvements and the emergence of international flights led to the creation of first commercial airlines after World War I and expanded between World Wars I and II. The oldest airline still in operation is KLM, the Dutch company founded in 1919. While some older airlines such as Air France (1933) and Delta Airlines (1925) still exist, others such as Pan American World Airways (1927–1991) and TWA (1925–2001) went bankrupt at the end of the twentieth century. At this time, air transport was developing mainly for freight, with companies such as l'Aéropostale in France. Passenger traffic was low, as air travel remained a luxury product.

1.1.2 1944–1978: The Emergence of Modern Air Transport

Until then reserved for a minority of passengers, constrained by still emerging technologies, and having no real legal framework to ensure its development, air transport had to wait until the end of the 1940s to develop. During World War II, hundreds of thousands of pilots were trained to fly, and just as many aircrafts were produced: the emerging airlines then offered them natural job opportunities. World War II also accelerated the launch of new technologies to make aircraft more maneuverable, faster, and safer. One of the main innovations was the invention of the jet engine, which was adapted for civil aircraft such as the De Havilland Comet (1949), the Caravelle (1957) and the Boeing 707 (1957). A few decades later, the Boeing 737 (in 1967) and the Boeing 747 (in 1969) considerably changed the on-board experience for passengers, enabling them to fly further while reducing unit costs.

This rapid expansion after World War II would not have been possible without the creation of a proper international legal framework. In 1944, 54 countries met in Chicago to sign the "Convention on International Civil Aviation," known as the "Chicago Convention." This convention laid the foundation for the development of international air transport (e.g., navigation, safety, overflight rights) and led to the creation of a specialized agency, the International Civil Aviation Organization (ICAO), which reports to the United Nations.

The combination of all these factors contributed to the rapid expansion of air traffic, which grew at an annual rate of approximately 10% until the end of the 1970s. While technology no longer impeded the development of aviation, the market remained highly fragmented, for regulatory reasons: each national airline enjoyed a legal monopoly in its domestic market, while international routes were heavily regulated, forcing airlines to sell their seats at prices set during international negotiations under the supervision of the International Air Transport Association (IATA).

1.1.3 1978–1997: The Beginnings of Air Transport Liberalization

From the end of the 1970s onward, the liberalization of air transport turned the sector upside down. It all began in the United States with the Airline Deregulation Act enacted by President Jimmy Carter in 1978. This law led to the opening up of many domestic routes to competition, allowing all US airlines to serve all routes within the United States, while being free to set their own prices and quantities.

This liberalization movement inspired the Europeans, who introduced several regulation "packages" from 1987 onward, also to gradually open up air transport to competition. It was the "third European package" that marked the real opening up of air transport to competition, guaranteeing the freedom to set price and seat availability on air routes within Europe. Passed in 1992, this third package came into force in 1997, making the European Union one of the most open air transport markets in the world.

This opening up to competition challenged local and national monopolies, as new players entered both the American and European markets and new routes were created. This led to a drastic drop in airfares (see Fig. 1.1). Thus, from 1978 (just before liberalization in the United States) to 2000 (just after liberalization in Europe), the average real (i.e., inflation-adjusted) price of a plane ticket reduced by more than half, due to both technological developments and intensified competition.

1.1.4 1997–2020: The Democratization of Air Transport

The liberalization of air transport in Europe and the United States led to greater competitive pressure on airlines. Previously preserved by a protective framework, incumbent airlines now had to face new players. To survive, they began forging

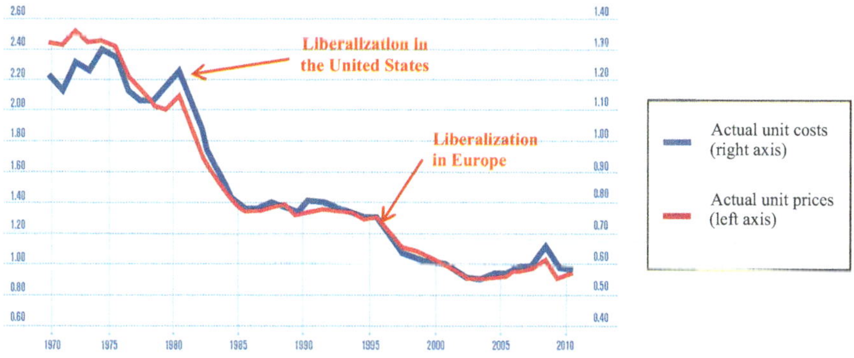

Fig. 1.1 Price trends and real unit costs since 1970. Source: Adapted from IATA (2011)

alliances or merging. In some cases, their survival was at stake: many airlines went bankrupt or shuttered, unable to survive the new competitive landscape.

In Europe, this exacerbated competition took place on two levels. First, on short- and medium-haul routes (up to 4-h flight time), incumbent airlines began facing competition from low-cost carriers such as Ryanair and EasyJet, whose market share kept growing every year. In 2023, low-cost carriers accounted for approximately 40% of the European market. This new competitive landscape meant lower ticket prices and a more uniform customer experience. Air travel was becoming a commodity, that is, a standardized product of known quality for which price was the main criterion of choice.

Second, on long-haul flights, such as intercontinental flights, competition mainly shifted with the arrival of the Gulf carriers Emirates, Qatar Airways, and Etihad Airways. While their prices were generally lower than those offered by European airlines, the quality of on-board services was often equivalent or better. These airlines contributed to the democratization of long-haul air transport and posed a real threat to European airlines, which make most of their profits on long-haul markets. This increased competition, on both short- and medium-haul routes, drove global air transport growth of more than 4% a year.

On average, during the period 2000–2020, the number of air passengers worldwide doubled, representing an average annual growth rate of 5%. Air travel was no longer a luxury product but was becoming accessible to many people. A study by Chiambaretto et al. (2022) shows that 91% of French people over the age of 25 have flown at least once in their lives and that more than 60% flew at least once a year in 2019. Another explanation lies in the strong growth of the middle class in emerging countries (particularly Asia), which has not only increased the number of air passengers but also shifted the center of air transport eastward. On the eve of the COVID-19 crisis, according to ICAO figures, more than 4.5 billion passengers flew worldwide in 2019.

1.1.5 Since 2020: A New Era, with New Challenges

At a time when air traffic growth seemed unstoppable, the COVID-19 pandemic brought the airline's development to a sudden and unprecedented halt. With air traffic contracting by more than 95% during the confinement, and an average 60% drop in the number of passengers carried worldwide in 2020 (1.8 billion passengers carried in 2020 vs. 4.5 billion in 2019), air transport experienced its biggest shock since World War II.

This crisis jeopardized the financial health of airlines, which sustained reductions in schedules during the confinements. Not all airlines were affected in the same way though. For example, low-cost carriers, which were in better financial health at the start of the crisis, as they have a cost structure with lower fixed than variable costs (as we discuss in Chap. 4), took advantage of the crisis. They were able to cut expenses more sharply during the months of confinement, while benefiting more quickly from the upturn in traffic, since their network is essentially intra-European and the first flights to resume were short- and medium-haul. In a way, low-cost airlines were the main winners of the crisis and saw their market share grow even more strongly over the next few years (Bréchemier & Combe, 2020).

While the COVID-19 crisis was unprecedented in terms of duration, intensity, and geographic scope, it is not the first crisis in the air transport industry. Economic crises (e.g., the oil crisis, the bursting of the dot-com bubble, the subprime mortgage crisis), geopolitical crises (e.g., the Gulf Wars, the terrorist attacks of September 11, 2001), and epidemics (e.g., severe acute respiratory syndrome) had already hit the air transport sector, but without any lasting impact on its growth.

Although air transport regained its pre-crisis traffic levels in 2024, the aviation sector emerged profoundly transformed by the crisis. Over a span of 5 years, air passenger behavior partially shifted, particularly among business travelers, who increasingly replaced air travel with videoconferencing. Moreover, the COVID-19 crisis accelerated awareness of the environmental challenges associated with air transport, contributing to the rise of "flight shame," or the guilt associated with flying.

However, the crisis had an impact on more than just passenger behavior. It reshaped the competitive landscape among airlines, widening the gap between low-cost carriers—undisputed winners of the crisis—and traditional airlines. Aircraft manufacturers' production and supply chains were also severely disrupted and, as of 2024, had yet to return to pre-crisis production rates.

While the COVID-19 crisis has now mostly passed, its effects have left the aviation sector profoundly and enduringly transformed.

1.2 Determinants of Air Transport Trends

Although air transport has experienced an upward trend in the number of passengers carried since World War II, steady growth has not always been the case (Fig. 1.2). Thus, what structural factors influence traffic trends? This question is particularly important for players in the air transport ecosystem that must forecast traffic over several years or even several decades. This is the case for major airports, which often must resize their terminals and runways to accommodate traffic. Likewise, aircraft manufacturers such as Airbus and Boeing pay close attention to changes in passenger numbers, notably to anticipate aircraft order volumes in different regions of the world and develop new aircraft models, with greater or lesser capacity.

Air traffic trends depend on a large number of factors, including economic, geopolitical, social, and demographic. Some are exogenous, making them difficult to predict, such as the COVID-19 crisis in 2020 or a war, such as that between Russia and Ukraine. Others are structural factors, which are more stable over time, making it possible to establish a causal and predictable relationship to air traffic. Among structural factors, two economic ones often used in traffic forecasts are the economic growth rate and the evolution of ticket prices.

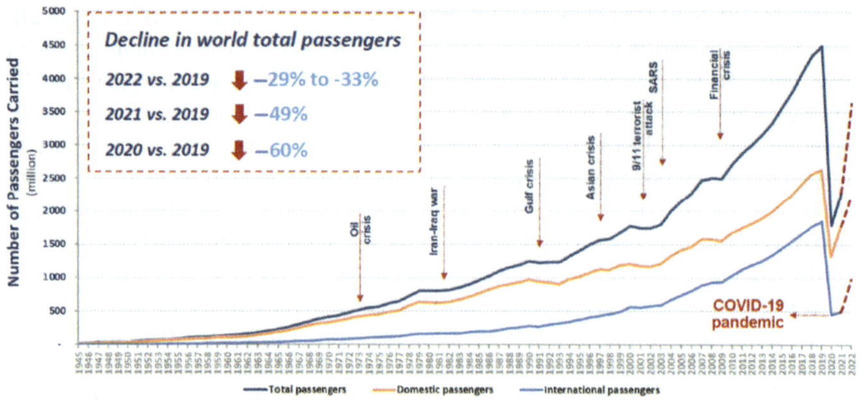

Fig. 1.2 World passenger traffic trends (1945–2021). Source: Adapted from ICAO (2022)

1.2.1 The Role of Economic Growth and Gross Domestic Product Per Capita

The total volume of passengers carried depends on a first economic variable: a country's wealth. We can assume that the richer a country is, the more likely its inhabitants are to travel by air, as air transport is a "superior good" (see Box 1.1). For example, in a country like Singapore, the number of trips per inhabitant is 4.6 per year, compared with 0.03 for a country like Togo. Since a country's wealth is usually measured by its gross domestic product (GDP), economic growth (i.e., an increase in GDP) should translate into an increase in air traffic.

Empirical studies show that the income elasticity of air transport (i.e., air transport's sensitivity of demand to changes in income) is always greater than 1, whatever the reason for travel, the length of the flight, or the region of the world. This means that an increase in GDP is a driver of growth for air travel. And an income elasticity greater than 1 means that air transport growth will usually be higher than that of the GDP. Symmetrically, a recession will have a negative impact on air transport, notably because tourists will refrain from traveling and companies will limit corporate travel. More specifically, three conclusions emerge from the empirical studies:

- income elasticity is higher for leisure customers than for business customers, at between 1.6 and 1.8 according to the US Civil Aviation Authority model for tourists. In other words, when a country's GDP rises by 1%, demand for leisure air travel increases by 1.6% to 1.8%;
- income elasticity is higher on long-haul flights than on short- and medium-haul flights. One explanation for this difference is that the richer consumers become, the farther they tend to travel; and
- income elasticity is higher in developing and emerging countries than in developed countries, due to a catch-up effect.

Box 1.1 Income elasticity and price elasticity

Microeconomic theory establishes a relationship between income and consumption structure by classifying different goods (and services) by their income elasticity. Income elasticity refers to the ratio of the percentage change in consumption of good X to the percentage change in income. Income elasticity is written as

$$\varepsilon = \frac{\frac{dQ_x}{Q_x}}{\frac{dI}{I}}$$

where Q_x is consumption of good X before the increase in income, I is income, and d is absolute change.

Three cases of income elasticity can be distinguished:

1. If elasticity is negative, an increase in income results in a drop in consumption of good X: here, we're talking about an inferior good. For example, if a consumer's income increases by 10%, he or she may reduce consumption of bread by 10% and switch to other food products such as rice.
2. If elasticity is positive and between 0 and 1, an increase in income leads to a small increase in consumption of good X: this refers to a normal good. For example, if a consumer's income increases by 10%, he or she will increase consumption of meat by 5%.
3. If elasticity is positive and greater than unity, an increase in income induces a more than proportional increase in the consumption of good X: this refers to a superior good. For example, when a consumer's income rises by 10%, his or her consumption of cinema and entertainment increases by 20%.

In parallel, price elasticity includes the relative reaction of demand for a good X to a (small) relative variation in its price, which is written as

$$c = \frac{\frac{dQ_x}{Q_x}}{\frac{dP_x}{P_x}}$$

where Q_X is the quantity of good X requested, P_X is the price of good X, and d is the absolute change.

For most products and services, the price elasticity is negative because the demand tends to decrease when prices go up. The more negative the price elasticity, the more the demand will be sensitive to price variations. If the value of price elasticity is between 0 and −1, the quantity demanded of good X decreases less proportionally than its price. In this case, demand is considered price inelastic.

If the value of the elasticity is smaller than −1, the quantity demanded of good X falls more sharply than the price rises. This is referred to as the price-elastic demand.

The role of a country's wealth in air traffic growth can be broken down into two distinct effects:

1. *A volume effect*: GDP can rise because the country's population increases. With a constant GDP per capita, an increase in population should automatically lead to an increase in traffic. Gillen et al. (2008) show that on the US market, the elasticity of air traffic to population varies between 0.5 and 1.8, depending on the methodology used.
2. *A wealth effect*: if a country's production grows faster than its population, its per capita wealth increases, which can lead people to travel more. In particular, in emerging countries such as China, GDP per capita has risen sharply during the last 20 years: from US$1050 in 2001 to US$12,600 in 2023, a 12-fold increase. This rise in living standards has led to the emergence of a vast urban "middle class" of more than 400 million people, who aspire to travel. This increase in air travel in China first developed on the domestic market, with a growth of 8% per year, before also taking off internationally. Projections for per capita GDP growth up to 2035 suggest that air travel in China will be quite strong, along with the increase in the Chinese middle class to 800 million people.

The impact of wealth per capita on air traffic is not linear, but rather asymptotic (Fig. 1.3). Thus, below a certain level of GDP per capita, air traffic remains low because the level of wealth of the population is too low to afford air travel. Then, when a country becomes an emerging nation, it experiences a high rate of economic growth, with a catch-up effect on air traffic trends. When the country has caught up, air traffic increases little, as the majority of people are already traveling significantly.

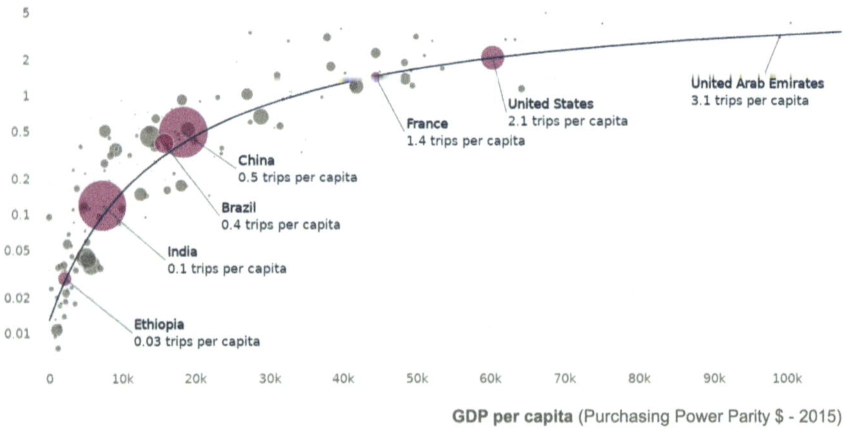

Fig. 1.3 The relationship between air traffic growth and GDP per capita. Source: Airbus (2024)

1.2.2 The Evolution of Airfare

The second economic factor influencing air traffic growth is ticket price. The expected relationship between airfare and air traffic is negative: when the average ticket price decreases, the number of passengers carried increases; symmetrically, an increase in the average ticket price leads to a decrease in demand.

How sensitive is demand to a change in ticket price? To answer this question, we need to estimate the price elasticity of demand (see Box 1.1): if the price elasticity of demand is very negative (i.e., less than −1), demand for air transport will react strongly to a change in ticket price. Symmetrically, if the price elasticity of demand is between 0 and −1 (i.e., close to 0), demand for air travel will not be sensitive to variations in ticket price.

Several studies (e.g., Gillen et al., 2008) have calculated the price elasticity of demand, distinguishing between the reason for travel (leisure or business), the duration of the flight (medium-/long-haul), the region of the world, and the level of analysis used (the route, the country, and the continent). Three conclusions emerge:

1. Price elasticity is always higher in absolute terms (i.e., a price increase will lead to a greater drop in demand) for leisure customers than for business customers, whatever the length of the flight. For example, price elasticity is −1.52 (in absolute terms) on medium-haul routes for leisure customers, meaning that a 1% increase in ticket price will result in a 1.52% drop in demand. For business travelers, by contrast, price elasticity is of the order of −0.7, such that a 1% price increase will lead only to a 0.7% drop in demand. A reason for this difference is that, unlike business travelers, whose tickets are often paid for by their employers, leisure passengers pay for their own air tickets and therefore are more sensitive to price variations.
2. Price elasticity is higher (in absolute terms) on medium-haul than long-haul routes, whatever the reason for travel. This is because people can substitute for air travel on national or regional flights; for example, they can take the car or train if airfares are too expensive. Conversely, these substitutes are less likely on long-haul routes, notably for reasons of trip duration.
3. Price elasticity varies widely around the world. Gillen et al. (2008) show that it is very high in Europe, which can be explained by strong competition between low-cost and incumbent airlines, with a value of −1.96 at route level. By contrast, in sub-Saharan Africa, price elasticity at the route level is only −0.9, as low-cost airlines are less developed and passengers are more captive to the few airlines serving these countries.

After we have an estimate of price and revenue elasticities, we can calculate the evolution of air traffic on the basis of two variables: GDP and the average price of air transport. Thus, the ICAO econometric model establishes the following relationship between the number of passenger–kilometers transported (PKT), the GDP, and the unit revenue per passenger (UR), over the period 1975–2005 and on worldwide traffic:

$$\mathrm{Ln}(\mathrm{PKT}) = 5.43 + 1.30\ln(\mathrm{GDP}) - 0.67\ln(\mathrm{UR}),$$

where Ln stands for logarithm

This statistically significant relationship shows that air transport growth depends strongly and positively on GDP (+1.30) and negatively on ticket price (–0.67). We note that the impact of GDP is twice as strong as that of the ticket price: this means that, in a simple two-variable model, GDP explains two-thirds of air traffic growth worldwide.

1.2.3 The Role of Air Transport Substitutes

While demand for air travel depends on macroeconomic factors, such as GDP, or factors specific to the airline industry, such as ticket prices, it is also influenced by the presence of substitutes for air travel. Depending on the distance traveled or the motive for traveling, two main substitutes are high-speed rail and videoconferencing. We focus here on high-speed rail and discuss videoconferencing further in Chap. 5 on new travel behavior.

In Europe since the 1990s and in Asia (particularly Japan and China) since the 2000s, governments have invested heavily in the construction of high-speed rail lines, enabling trains to travel at speeds faster than 300 km/h. The strong development of these lines and the expansion of high-speed train services (e.g., TGV in France, ICE in Germany, Shinkansen in Japan) have resulted in the development of credible alternatives to air travel on certain short- and medium-haul routes.

By offering city-to-city routes at prices equivalent to or sometimes lower than air travel, high-speed rail has become a strong competitor to airlines on domestic and some international routes. As Fig. 1.4 shows, high-speed rail's market share rises (to the detriment of air travel) when train journey times are less than 3 h. For example, routes initially offered by air, including Paris–Brussels, Milano–Roma, and Barcelona–Madrid, have disappeared in favor of rail. For journeys of between 3 and 5 h by train, rail and air are in head-to-head competition, and market shares between the two modes of transport are relatively balanced. This is the case, for example, on routes such as Paris–Montpellier and Paris–Marseille. Finally, when train journey times exceed 4 h, air travel again gains over rail, offering significantly shorter journey times. This is the case, for example, on a route such as Paris–Nice, where the plane remains more attractive to passengers than the train, which takes almost 5 h (vs. 1 h by plane).

The magnitude of substitutability between air and rail is measured by a specific indicator: cross-price elasticity. Cross-price elasticity measures the impact of a price variation for product A (e.g., train) on demand for product B (e.g., plane). If the cross-price elasticity is positive, the two products are substitutable: when the price of one product rises, demand shifts toward the other. For example, on the Spanish market, Hortelano et al. (2016) showed that a 1% increase in the price of

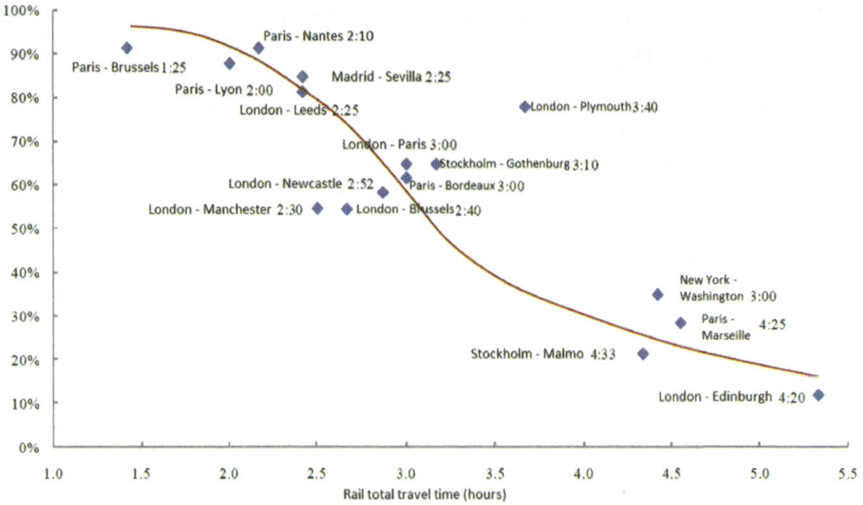

Fig. 1.4 Train market share as a function of train journey time. Source: Xia and Zhang (2016)

high-speed rail increased the probability of choosing air travel on an equivalent route by 69%.

However, the idea of substitutability between air and rail is debatable: in some cases, these two means of transport are rather complementary. For example, air and rail operators are increasingly offering air and rail tickets as part of an intermodal "air + rail" package. These combined tickets allow passengers to book their train and plane tickets with a single reservation. These multimodal solutions enable airlines to offer their passengers a greater number of destinations (served only by train).

While macroeconomic factors can influence the dynamics of air transport, the relationship can also work in the opposite direction. That is, air transport can contribute to economic development.

1.3 The Weight and Economic Impact of Air Transport

To fully understand the weight and impact of air transport on an economy, we first need to understand the mechanisms through which air transport and the economy interact. Then, we can assess the weight of air transport in the economy, whether in terms of GDP share or employment, on a static basis. Finally, we supplement this analysis with a dynamic approach to measure the impact of air transport growth on various economic indicators (e.g., GDP, employment, attractiveness).

1.3.1 The Relationship Between the Economy and Air Transport

The economy and air transport influence each other through a multitude of flows. Zhang and Graham (2020) characterized all these flows as shown in Fig. 1.5.

First, airports and airlines make decisions about network, capacity, fares, and schedules based on profitability expectations (shaded square). These decisions characterize the supply side of the air transport system (link 1), which in turn influences the cost and demand for travel (link 2). Variations in demand, in turn, affect the profitability of the aviation sector (link 3). Links (1)–(2) and (3) thus delimit the internal feedback loop linking supply and demand in the air transport system.

Second, links (4)–(5) and (6) focus on the interactions between the economy and the air transport system. Employment and spending in the aviation industry have direct, indirect, and induced impacts on the economy (link 4). Direct impacts arise from activities directly linked to air transport operations. Indirect impacts come from companies supplying goods and services to the upstream supply chain, such as aviation fuel suppliers, aircraft component suppliers, and infrastructure construction companies. Induced impacts include subsequent spending by households directly or indirectly employed by the aviation industry itself. We refer to the sum of direct, indirect, and induced impacts as "supply chain effects."

Third, the supply of air transport stimulates certain types of activities and facilitates the growth of other industries (link 5). Air transport boosts productivity, facilitates global trade, promotes tourism, improves the efficiency of supply chains, and enables investment and labor supply within and outside countries and regions. These are the positive externalities ("spillover effects") of air transport on the economy.

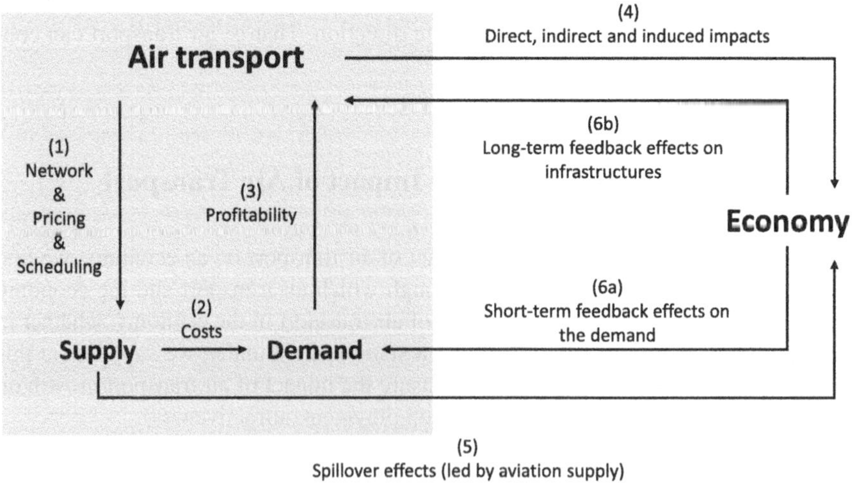

Fig. 1.5 Main interactions between air transport and the economy. Source: Adapted from Zhang and Graham (2020)

Finally, we note the presence of feedback loops, where the economy has an impact on air transport. For example, in the short run, demand for passenger and freight air transport depends in part on the level of development and/or economic growth in a region (link 6a). In the long run, economic growth in a region generates capital and resources for infrastructure investment, which can trigger a series of secondary effects, stimulating all sectors of the economy, including air transport (link 6b).

1.3.2 The Impact of Air Transport: The Static Approach

Generally speaking, air transport has a fourfold impact on the economy:

1. A direct impact, generally assessed through the jobs and activities generated by airline and airport operations, aircraft maintenance, air traffic management, and local manufacturers;
2. An indirect impact, measured by the additional jobs and activities generated by suppliers to the aeronautics industry;
3. An induced impact, measured by the employment and activities generated by all the spending of people employed directly or indirectly in the air transport sector; and
4. A catalytic impact, measured in terms of jobs and revenues generated by the airport in the region and other sectors (e.g., productivity, new business start-ups).

As the catalytic impact is rather difficult to measure, empirical studies focus mainly on the first three impact categories (Zhang & Graham, 2020). These categories are based on the concept of "multiplier," which evaluates the impact of one expenditure (e.g., an air passenger who sleeps in a hotel) on other expenditures in the region (e.g., expenditure from the income of the hotel's employees or suppliers). The multiplier (M) evaluates the positive spin-offs generated by the aeronautical industry and is measured as

$$M = \frac{Direct\ Impact + Indirect\ Impact + Induced\ Impact}{Direct\ Impact}.$$

Most studies show that the multiplier is greater than 1.3 and that the value of the multiplier increases with the size of the metropolitan area in which the airport is located (Brathen & Halpern, 2012).

On a global scale, ICAO (2020) shows that, with a total impact of more than US$2700 billion, air transport accounted for over 3.6% of global GDP in 2019, while employing more than 65 million people worldwide (see Fig. 1.6). With regard to the different types of impact, we see that the direct impact in terms of GDP is more than €700 billion, or 26% of its total impact. In terms of jobs, aviation generates more than 10 million direct jobs, or 15% of all the jobs it helps to create, directly or indirectly.

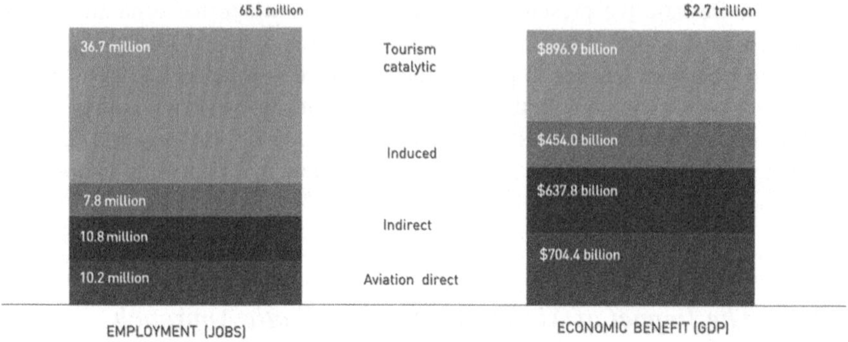

Fig. 1.6 Economic and employment contribution of air transport worldwide (2019). Source: ICAO (2020)

However, the weight and economic impact of air transport can vary greatly from country to country. In a country heavily dependent on tourism (and, therefore, on air connections), aviation and air transport will play a more important role in its economy. In 2014, for example, air transport accounted for 26.7% of Dubai's GDP. Similarly, island countries will, at equivalent levels of economic development, make greater use of the air and sea to transport passengers. In these countries, the economic weight of air transport generally exceeds 10% of GDP, as it is an essential mode of transport for the accessibility and opening up of certain isolated islands.

1.3.3 The Impact of Air Transport: The Dynamic Approach

Many local authorities provide financial support for airlines to serve their city or region because they expect it to boost their local economic development. To what extent does the opening of new air routes or capacity have an impact on local economic growth?

1.3.3.1 Air Transport and Economic Growth: Correlation or Causation?

For many years, studies analyzing the link between air transport and economic development have shown a strong correlation between the two (Zhang & Graham, 2020). However, until the early 2000s, most studies had observed a co-evolution between air transport and economic development, without clearly indicating the direction of causality. Only since the early 2000s have studies and articles analyzed the causality between the two concepts, using, for example, Granger causality tests.[2]

[2]The Granger causality test exploits the temporal order in a time series and assumes that effects cannot occur before causes. There are different types of Granger causality test, but whatever type

The majority of these studies confirmed that air transport led to economic growth and not the other way round.

However, recent research has shown that the reality is more complex. Some studies (e.g., Baker et al., 2015) have found a feedback effect of economic growth on air transport, showing a cumulative link between economic activity and air passengers, thus generating a virtuous circle for the most connected regions. In the same vein, Mukkala and Tervo's (2013) study reveals that the direction of causality depends on the status of the region. In central regions (i.e., the most developed ones), the path runs from economic growth to air transport. In other words, it is because these regions are wealthy, with high business and economic activity, that many airlines want to serve these attractive markets. In peripheral (i.e., less developed) regions, by contrast, the presence of air transport stimulates economic growth by reducing transport costs and improving regional connectivity.

1.3.3.2 The Impact of Air Transport on Economic Development

To analyze the economic impact of air transport, several factors are considered, including regional GDP growth, business location decisions, local investment, employment, wages, and regional demographic trends (Fig. 1.7).

Air transport significantly influences regional GDP by enhancing connectivity, which lowers transportation costs and facilitates international trade, investment, and tourism. Studies such as those by ACI (2015) and PwC (2014) show that increased airport connectivity and capacity lead to measurable GDP growth. For example, a 10% increase in airport connectivity can raise local GDP by 0.5%, and a similar increase in seat capacity might boost GDP by 1% (PwC, 2014).

The presence of airports also affects corporate decisions about where to establish operations. Improved air transport links reduce transaction costs and make it easier to access international markets, which is particularly attractive to high-tech start-ups and multinational companies. Research by Bel and Fageda (2008) indicates that enhanced intercontinental flight availability can increase local corporate headquarters by 4%.

Furthermore, air transport contributes to job creation and higher wages in the region. It attracts skilled employees and fosters technology and knowledge transfer, positively impacting local economies. Green (2007) observed that a 10% rise in flights per capita can result in a 2.8% increase in jobs, with even higher growth in hub cities.

In addition, better air transport facilities can drive demographic growth by making regions more attractive to potential residents, especially in hub cities where population growth rates are significantly higher. Blonigen and Cristea (2015) found that a 10% increase in air passengers correlates with a population increase of up to 0.9%.

---

is used, the philosophy remains the same.

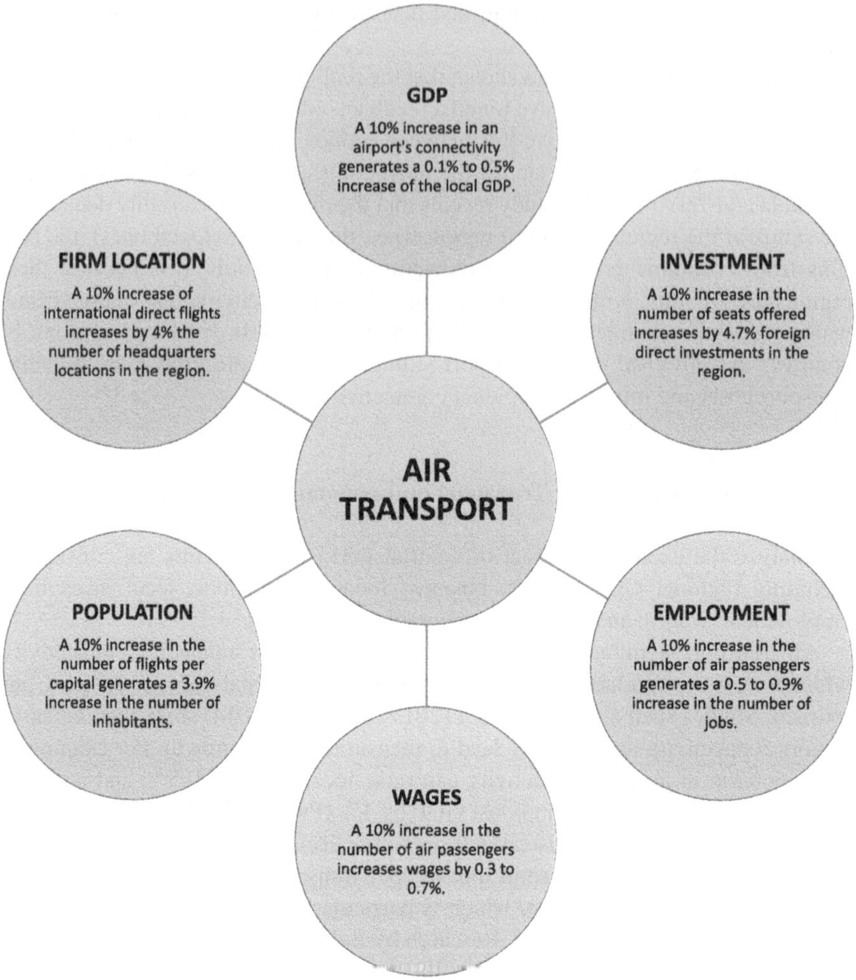

Fig. 1.7 Main results on the impact of air transport on economic development. Source: The authors

References

ACI. (2015). *The impact of an airport.*

Airbus. (2024). *Global Market Forecast 2024-2043.*

Baker, D., Merkert, R., & Kamruzzaman, M. (2015). Regional aviation and economic growth: cointegration and causality analysis in Australia. *Journal of Transport Geography, 43*, 140–150.

Bel, G., & Fageda, X. (2008). Getting there fast: Globalization, intercontinental flights and location of headquarters. *Journal of Economic Geography, 8*(4), 471–495.

Blonigen, B., & Cristea, A. (2015). Air service and urban growth: Evidence from a quasi-natural policy experiment. *Journal of Urban Economics, 86*, 128–146.

Bråthen, S., & Halpern, N. (2012). Air transport service provision and management strategies to improve the economic benefits for remote regions. *Research in Transportation Business & Management, 4*, 3–12.

Bréchemier, D., & Combe, E. (2020). *After Covid-19, air transportation in Europe: The time for decision making*. Fondapol.

Chiambaretto, P., Bildstein, C., Alessandra, P., Rouyre, A., Feiereisen, S., Fernandez, A.-S., Seran, T., & Chappert, H. (2022). La génération Z et le transport aérien: quelles différences entre les 15-24 ans et le reste de la population française? *Les Carnets de la Chaire Pégase*, n°4.

Gillen, D., Morrison, W., & Stewart, C. (2008). *Air travel demand elasticities: Concepts, issues and measurement*. Government of Canada, Department of Finance.

Green, R. (2007). Airports and economic development. *Real Estate Economics, 35*(1), 91–112.

Hortelano, A. O., Guzman, A. F., Preston, J., & Vassallo, J. M. (2016). Price elasticity of demand on the high-speed rail lines of Spain: Impact of the new pricing scheme. *Transportation Research Record, 2597*(1), 90–98.

IATA. (2011). *Vision 2050.*

ICAO. (2020). *Aviation benefits report.*

ICAO. (2022). *Guidance on potential policies and coordinated approaches for the deployment of sustainable aviation fuels.*

Mukkala, K., & Tervo, H. (2013). Air transportation and regional growth: Which way does the causality run? *Environment and Planning A, 45*(6), 1508–1520.

PwC. (2014). *Connectivity and growth: Directions of travel for airport investments.*

Xia, W., & Zhang, A. (2016). High-speed rail and air transport competition and cooperation: A vertical differentiation approach. *Transportation Research Part B: Methodological, 94*, 456–481.

Zhang, F., & Graham, D. J. (2020). Air transport and economic growth: A review of the impact mechanism and causal relationships. *Transport Reviews, 40*(4), 506–528.

Chapter 2
The Air Transport Ecosystem and Its Regulation

Having described the main determinants and impacts of air transport, in this chapter we introduce the various players and the rules of the game. Airlines are part of an ecosystem with a multitude of players whose actions are constrained by a strict regulatory framework. In the first section, we identify the main players in this ecosystem, including aircraft and engine manufacturers, aircraft leasing companies, and, downstream, global distribution systems and airports. In the second part, we demonstrate that air transport is highly regulated by a set of sector-specific rules covering a wide range of areas: traffic rights, safety, flight security, and access to airport slots. Finally, in the third part, we show that, in addition to sector-specific rules, airlines are subject to competition regulations, whether in terms of cooperation between competitors, abuse of dominant position, or merger control.

2.1 The Air Transport Ecosystem and Value Chain

The air transport sector involves a multiplicity of operators with different levels of profitability (see Fig. 2.1, which does not include regulators, which we mention in the rest of the chapter). In this section, we present the main links in the air transport value chain (with the exception of airlines, which we address in greater details in Chaps. 3 and 4), before highlighting the differences in profitability between these different players.

P. Chiambaretto, E. Combe, *Introduction to Air Transport*, SpringerBriefs in Business, https://doi.org/10.1007/978-3-031-99936-9_2

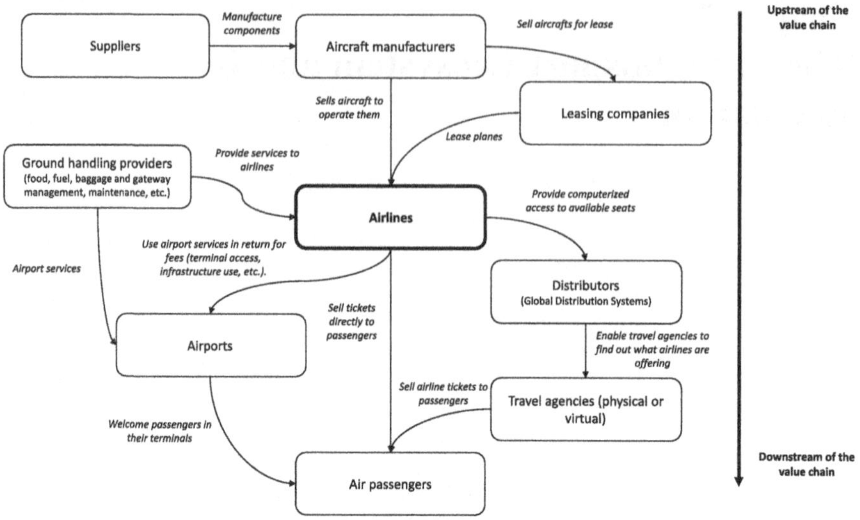

Fig. 2.1 The main players in the aviation ecosystem. Source: The authors

2.1.1 *Upstream: Aircraft Manufacturers*

To operate flights, an airline first needs an aircraft. In 2024, around 25,000 commercial aircrafts were flying around the world. From the 1950s to the 1970s, the United States was the world's only manufacturer of commercial aircrafts, with the Boeing, McDonnell Douglas, and Lockheed companies. Lockheed left the civil aircraft market in the 1980s to focus on military aircrafts, and McDonnell Douglas was acquired by Boeing in 1997. The Europeans entered the wide-body market with Airbus in the 1970s, which, with Boeing, progressively formed a global duopoly (Fig. 2.2). Today, these two companies account for a combined market share of more than 85%. Nevertheless, the recent difficulties encountered by Boeing in the past decades have led to an overall dominance of the commercial aircraft market by Airbus. For example, in 2024, Airbus delivered 770 aircrafts, representing more than 70% of the total deliveries. The remaining 15% is shared by other manufacturers, mainly offering regional aircrafts: Embraer (Brazil), Mitsubishi Aircraft Corporation (Japan), Sukhoi (Russia), and Bombardier (Canada), which in 2017 was acquired by Airbus.

Aircraft manufacturing requires the involvement of multiple suppliers and subcontractors, such as Safran, General Electric, Rolls Royce, Thalès, Liebherr Aerospace, Honeywell, Latecoère, Lockheed Martin, and Michelin. These firms supply aircraft components such as engines, seats, landing gear, electrical systems, tires, and more. They are also relatively specialized and few in number. For example, on a global scale, only three major engine manufacturers are in competition. The same applies to seats and tires. This small number of suppliers is due to the

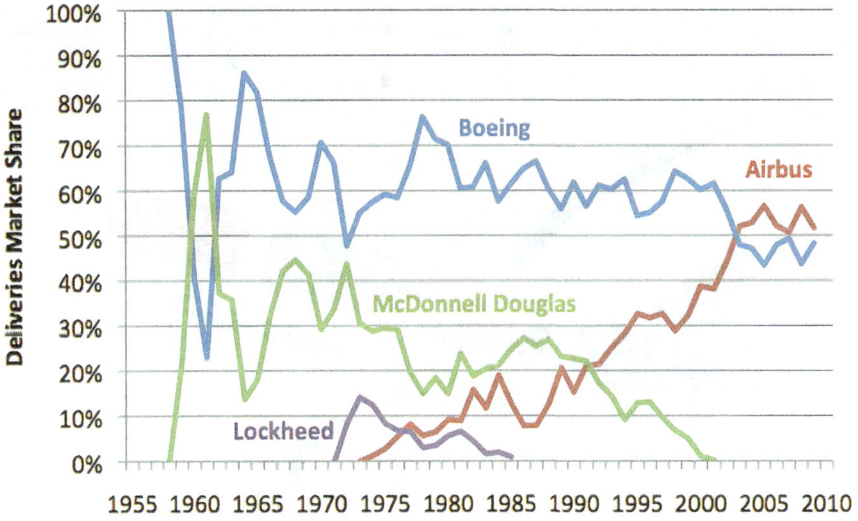

Fig. 2.2 Market share of civil aircraft deliveries. Source: Morrison et al. (2011)

existence of high entry barriers, for technological, legal, and capital-intensive reasons.

This oligopolistic market structure gives suppliers a high bargaining power over manufacturers such as Boeing and Airbus. Indeed, it is quite common to find the same parts from one supplier in two competing aircrafts. The growing role of suppliers is such that aircraft manufacturers are now seen less as manufacturers than as integrators of parts provided by different suppliers. The case of the Boeing 787 is rather telling in this respect: this aircraft is made up of multiple components from different companies located around the world, including Japan, France, Australia, and Canada (Fig. 2.3).

This increased subcontracting of production can lead to delays if suppliers cannot keep up with the production rhythms imposed by manufacturers. The stakes are all the more higher given that the world's fleet is set to double in size over the next 15 years, and annual production rates will have to rise accordingly by more than 15%.

2.1.2 Upstream: The Growing Role of Leasing Companies

Traditionally, most airlines owned their aircrafts. After purchasing an aircraft, the airline would then use it for 15–20 years before selling it on to begin a second life, usually with an airline in a developing country.

A growing proportion of airlines no longer own their aircrafts but lease them instead. In 2024, for the first time in the history of aviation, more than 50% of the

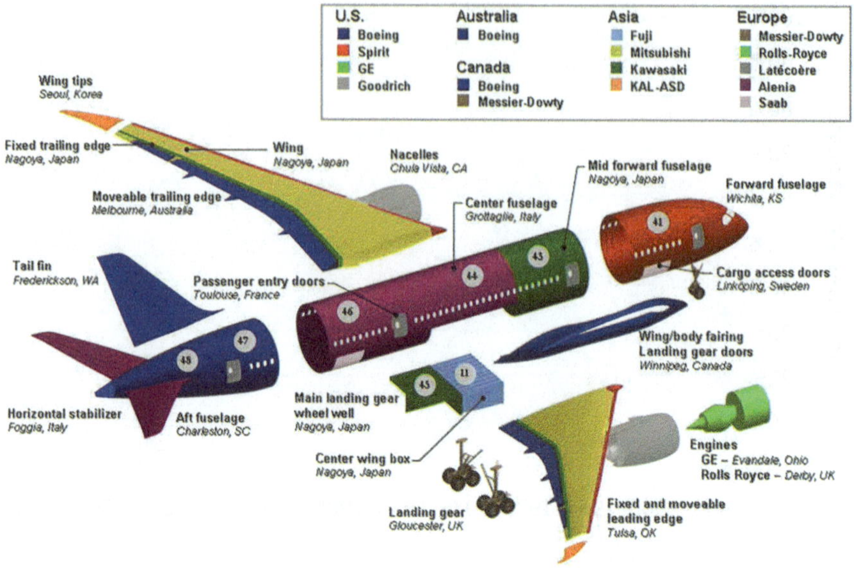

Fig. 2.3 The Boeing 787 as an assembly of components from around the world. Source: Moore et al. (2008)

world's fleet was leased, and this share is still growing. Unbeknownst to the general public, leasing companies own a large part of the global fleet, which they loan to airlines around the world. For example, in 2024, AerCap owned more than 1700 aircrafts, while an airline like Emirates operated around 260 aircrafts (a significant share of which were leased).

Three main reasons explain why many airlines prefer leasing to ownership. First, leasing gives airlines greater flexibility, enabling them to adapt the size and composition of their fleet to their needs. Second, leasing enables airlines to smooth out their investments over time and gradually pay for the operation of their aircrafts. Third, leasing enables airlines to renew their fleet more frequently (by leasing the most recent model each time): they benefit from new technologies and can offer a better passenger experience, while limiting operating costs (e.g., newer engines consume less fuel).

The development of leasing has had the effect of lowering the entry barriers for setting up an airline, since investing in the purchase of an aircraft is no longer necessary. "Wet leasing" an aircraft and the associated crew to operate it is even possible.

2.1.3 Downstream: Global Distribution Systems and Plane Ticket Distribution

In general, airline passengers have two options to buy a plane ticket: either directly from the airline (either on its website or at an airline agency) or through an intermediary such as a travel agency or an online comparator. For tickets bought directly from the airline, the airline has direct access to its "inventory" (i.e., all the tickets available for flights over the next 12 months). For tickets bought through a travel agency or flight comparator, these intermediaries do not have direct access to all the tickets offered by the airlines. As such, these intermediaries will ask other players, known as global distribution systems (GDSs), to find out what tickets are available from the airlines.

GDSs are platforms or intermediaries that continuously connect travel agencies (physical or virtual) to airlines, giving them access to seat availability and fares on different airline flights. The GDS business model involves charging travel agencies a commission for each airline ticket purchased.

There are many GDSs (with some only distributing tickets for airlines in a given country), but three main players share more than 95% of the global airline ticket distribution market: Amadeus (approx. 40–45%), Sabre (approx. 30%), and TravelPort (approx. 20%).

The role of GDSs has fluctuated over time. Initially created in the 1980s, GDSs' role diminished in the 2000s and again in the 2010s with the rise of low-cost airlines, which distributed their tickets exclusively via their own websites (and, therefore, without customers going through travel agencies or GDSs, thereby avoiding commissions and reducing ticket prices). Similarly, traditional airlines have sought to reduce their dependence on GDSs by promoting their own ticket distribution. In recent years, however, GDSs have again become more attractive, particularly since low-cost airlines are targeting business travelers whose bookings are made almost exclusively through travel agencies (and, therefore, GDSs).

2.1.4 Downstream: The Role of Airports

There are more than 40,000 airports worldwide, but only one-quarter of them handle commercial flights. For example, of France's 480 airfields, only 120 are operated commercially. Despite this large number of airports, air traffic is concentrated around just a few. In France, the two Paris airports (Paris Charles de Gaulle and Paris Orly) account for more than half of French air traffic, and the 15 largest French airports generate more than 95% of air traffic, sometimes creating airport congestion.

The global ranking of airports by passenger numbers highlights the importance of major hubs such as Atlanta, Dubai, and London Heathrow, as well as the rise of new airports such as Istanbul and New Delhi (Fig. 2.4).

2023	2022	2019	AIRPORT	2023	% CHANGE VS 2022	% CHANGE VS 2019
1	1	1	ATLANTA, USA (ATL)	104 653 451	11.7	-5.3
2	5	4	DUBAI, UAE (DXB)	86 994 365	31.7	0.7
3	2	10	DALLAS/FORT WORTH, USA (DFW)	81 755 538	11.4	8.9
4	8	7	LONDON, UK (LHR)	79 183 364	28.5	-2.1
5	16	5	TOKYO, JAPAN (HND)	78 719 302	55.1	-7.9
6	3	16	DENVER, USA (DEN)	77 837 917	12.3	12.8
7	7	28	ISTANBUL, TURKEY (IST)	76 027 321	18.3	45.7
8	6	3	LOS ANGELES, USA (LAX)	75 050 875	13.8	-14.8
9	4	6	CHICAGO, USA (ORD)	73 894 226	8.1	-12.7
10	9	17	NEW DELHI, INDIA (DEL)	72 214 841	21.4	5.4

* Total passengers enplaned and deplaned, passengers in transit counted once

Fig. 2.4 Worldwide airport ranking by passengers number (2019–2023). Source: ACI (2024)

This polarization of air traffic flows around just a few airports can be explained by, among other things, the diversity of airport types. This diversity of airports naturally leads to differences in business models (i.e., in terms of revenue sources and costs for airports), but some commonalities remain. In terms of revenues, there are first and foremost aeronautical revenues, which depend on activities linked to aircraft operations: passenger fees, landing fees, and parking fees. Second are non-aeronautical revenues, such as those generated by the airport's real estate, car parking, stores, and restaurants. On average, aeronautical revenues account for 55% of airport revenues, while non-aeronautical revenues account for 45% (with a downward trend due to the development of ride-hailing services and e-commerce).

Since airports regularly find themselves in a local monopoly situation, they may be tempted to set high charges to the detriment of airlines. To avoid any abuse, aeronautical charges are usually regulated by a public authority. The challenge for the regulator is to validate the level of charges proposed by airports, so as to enable them to operate profitably without jeopardizing the airlines. The setting of these fees is therefore the subject of intense negotiation and raises debates about the relevant scope of regulation (see Box 2.1).

Box 2.1 Single, dual, or adjusted till

Single till: a single till for all aeronautical and non-aeronautical services. Regulated airport charges are set to ensure a fair return on all capital invested in the fund.

Dual till: co-existence of an "aeronautical activities" till and a "non-aeronautical activities" till. The scope considered for regulation is limited to aeronautical activities and excludes revenues from non-aeronautical activities.

Adjusted till: an intermediate arrangement, with some commercial activities maintained within the regulated perimeter.

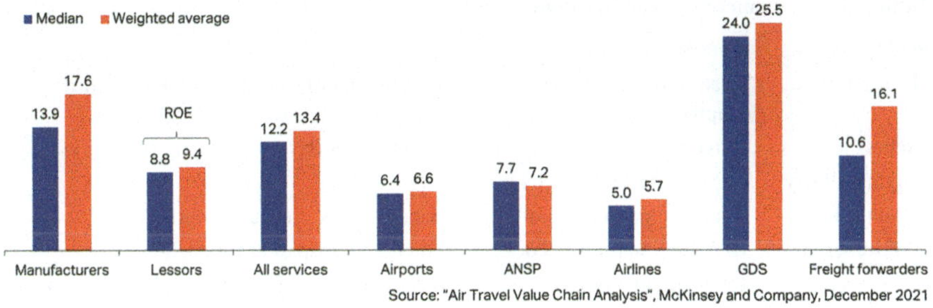

Fig. 2.5 ROIC of the various players in the air transport value chain. Source: IATA (2022)

The dual-till system can have the effect of driving up airport charges, because revenues generated by non-aeronautical revenues (which are generally the most profitable for an airport) are not taken into account when determining aeronautical charges. Airlines are therefore seeking a return to a single till (which does not underestimate airport revenues and leads to lower charges), while airport operators prefer regulation based on a dual or adjusted till.

Nevertheless, the relationship between airports and airlines is not limited to this conflicting vision. Well aware of their interdependence, airlines and airports are increasingly working to form partnerships to offer air passengers a more seamless experience.

In the airline industry, the profitability levels of the various players vary widely. Figure 2.5 shows the return on invested capital (ROIC) of the main players, with airlines, the core of this ecosystem, presenting the lowest levels of ROIC. These differences can be explained by the market structure. For example, some links in the value chain are duopolies (e.g., manufacturers) or oligopolies (e.g., GDSs), while others face stronger competition (e.g., airlines). The stronger the competition, the lower the returns on capital invested tend to be. Similarly, differences in returns can be explained by the structure of the players' costs and revenues. High fixed costs (for airline manufacturers) or low marginal costs (for GDSs) give some players a competitive advantage over new entrants.

2.2 Air Transport Regulation

Passenger air transport is heavily governed by a set of rules in many areas: though not exhaustive, these include rules on traffic rights, safety, flight security, access to airport slots, the transparency of information provided to consumers, and even liability in case of flight delays or cancellations (Table 2.1).

These rules are implemented and enforced by various public bodies at the international, regional, and national levels:

Table 2.1 The main rules in air transport

Rule	Purpose of the rule
Traffic rights	To authorize a foreign airline to overfly and/or operate a flight to a third country
Access to slots	To regulate slot shortages in congested airports
Flight security	To prevent illicit acts by passengers
Flight safety	To ensure proper aircraft maintenance; check crew capabilities
Consumer law	To ensure that ticket sales conditions are transparent for customers
Passenger rights	To ensure that passengers are protected in case of flight cancellations or delays

Source: The authors

1. At the international level, the ICAO, which was created in 1944 in the wake of the Chicago Convention, plays a central role. This agency's main mission is to draw up standards and recommendations to guarantee a uniform level of safety in air transport. In particular, it publishes the *Manual of International Air Transport Regulations*, which brings together all the ICAO's recommendations on air transport rules.
2. At the regional level, in Europe, air transport is regulated by various public institutions: the European Commission adopts directives and regulations on air transport, which are implemented by member states. Certain functions are pooled across Europe, such as the European Aviation Safety Agency (EASA) for air safety and Eurocontrol, in charge of air navigation.
3. At the national level are specialized administrations such as France's Direction Générale de l'Aviation Civile (DGAC) or Italy's Ente Nazionale per l'Aviazione Civile (ENAC). In the United States, the Federal Aviation Administration (FAA) is in charge of all matters related to air transport.

2.2.1 Regulating Traffic Rights

To operate flights, an airline must first obtain several authorizations. The first of these is the air operator's certificate, an approval issued for commercial transport operations. It is supplemented with an operating license, which establishes the commercial scope of operations allocated to the airline.

If an airline wishes to fly exclusively within its own country, it generally needs no additional authorization. If, alternatively, it desires to operate international flights, it will need to obtain "traffic rights": these rights allow the airline to land in the destination country and overfly the countries en route to that destination. These rights, often negotiated in the form of bilateral agreements, are broken down into rules known as "freedoms of the air." These rules, of which there are nine to date (see Fig. 2.6), have been codified since 1944 by the Chicago Convention. They combine to form an agreement of "traffic rights," the scope of which can be more or less extensive.

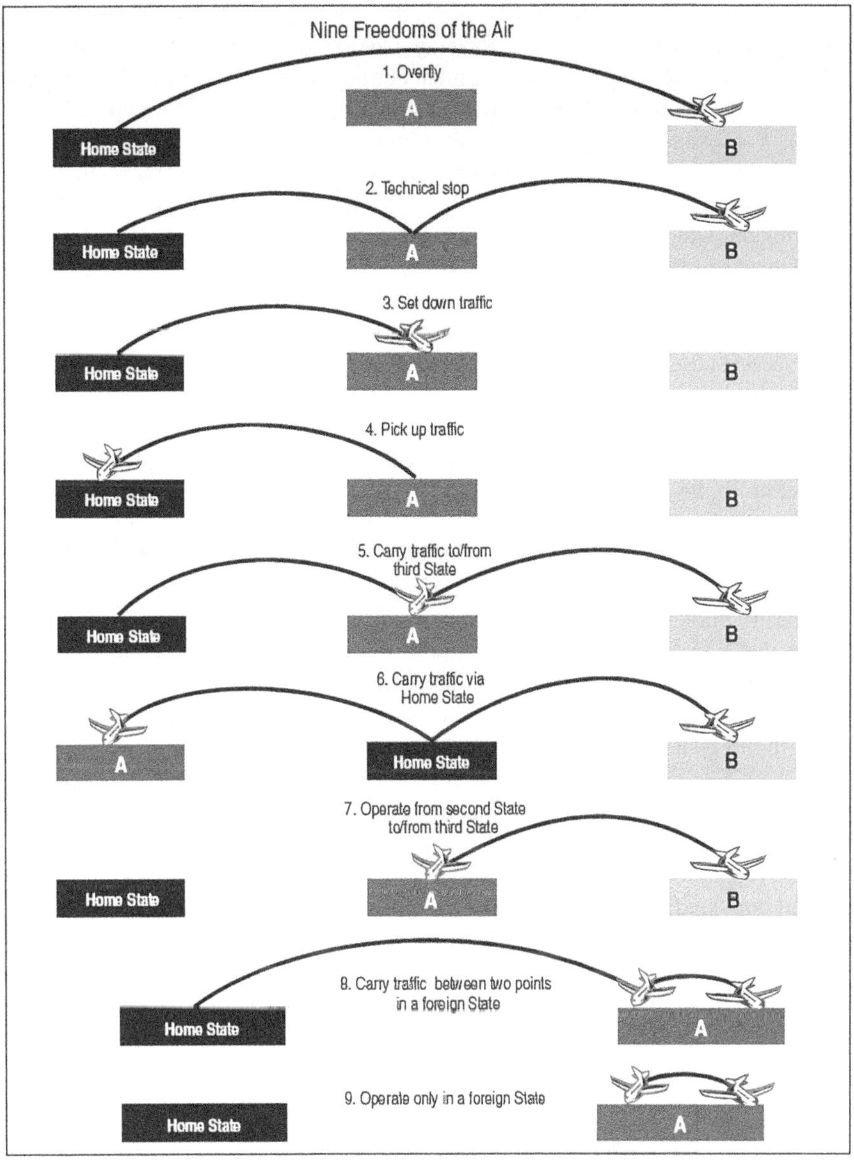

Fig. 2.6 The nine freedoms of the air. Source: ICAO (2013)

First, the most common case is when two countries negotiate traffic rights covering several of the nine freedoms, but without going as far as complete traffic liberalization. Such a bilateral agreement is the result of lengthy negotiations, combining different and sometimes conflicting objectives: to promote commercial and passenger traffic between the two countries, notably with a view to developing tourism; to avoid jeopardizing the competitiveness of the flag carrier if the airline of the other country has a strong competitive advantage; and to be in a state of diplomatic relations with the other county. The agreement defines precisely the frequency of flights per week, the landing and stopover points, the possibility of creating alliances, and so on. For example, the bilateral air transport agreement between China and Germany currently regulates the number of weekly passenger and cargo flights. At the beginning of 2024, China initiated an expansion of these quotas with the German government, which led to a new deal: in the summer of 2025, Chinese airlines will be allowed to offer four additional passenger flights per week to Germany and an additional four in the fall. In return, German airlines will receive 17 additional cargo flights per week to China.

A second case is an "open-skies" agreement, covering the first seven freedoms, with no limit on the number of flights. More than 400 open-skies agreements have been signed worldwide. For example, in 2007, Europe and the United States signed an open-skies agreement that, among other things, allows European Union airlines to operate flights to the United States from any European airport, with no restrictions on the number of flights.

A third case is when countries grant each other all nine freedoms set out in the Chicago Convention. This configuration is quite rare, occurring mainly within the European Union since 1997. In particular, the liberalization of European airspace means that a European airline from country A can operate flights within a foreign country, without continuing the flight to its own country, which corresponds to the ninth freedom of the air. An Irish airline like Ryanair, for example, can operate as many flights as it likes in the Italian domestic market.

It should be noted that traffic rights between two countries can be suspended, particularly during wartime. This has been the case since February 2022 between the European Union and Russia: European airspace has been closed to Russian airlines, in retaliation for Moscow's invasion of Ukraine. In concrete terms, no Russian aircraft may land, take off, or fly over EU territory, though some flights, notably for humanitarian purposes, may be authorized. The situation is of course symmetrical: Russian airspace is closed to European airlines, forcing them to modify their routes to operate flights to Asia, extending flight times by several hours and increasing operating costs significantly.

2.2.2 *Slot Control*

For an airline from country A to have the right to fly to an airport in country B, it must obtain a *slot*, that is, the authorization to take off from or land at this airport within a given time slot (usually 10 min) on a given day. The slot, granted by public authorities, confers a right of use but does not, in itself, constitute a property right.

At so-called secondary airports, a large number of slots are available throughout the day, so the opening of a new route by an airline is rather easy: all that is required is the submission of a flight schedule after the operating permit has been obtained.

The situation is quite different in congested major airports, such as Schiphol in Amsterdam or Heathrow in London: the number of slots offered is lower than the number requested by airlines, particularly in the most attractive hub periods—morning and evening. For example, since 1994, the number of slots at Paris Orly airport has been limited to 250,000, with a curfew from 11.30 PM to 6 AM, even though demand for slots is much higher.

Given this scarcity of slots, an administrative system has been set up in Europe, known as "coordination." Regulation 95/93 requires each European Union member state to grant a national authority the task of managing available slots, in compliance with three fundamental principles: transparency of procedure, neutrality, and non-discrimination.

Four main rules govern slot allocation:

- *The "grandfather rule"*: a carrier that has already operated a slot can claim the same slot for the following season. This rather conservative rule gives a decisive advantage to traditional airlines at major airports.
- *The 80% rule, also known as the "use it or lose it" rule*: an air carrier must use at least 80% of a slot it holds during a scheduling season. If it does not, the slot is taken back and redistributed to other airlines the following season. This rule can sometimes lead to undesirable effects: during the COVID-19 crisis, given the collapse in air traffic, some airlines threatened to fly and did fly their planes empty to keep their slots for the following season. This situation led the European Commission to temporarily relax the 80% rule, lowering the threshold to 40%.
- *The 50/50 rule*: free slots (whether due to 80% non-utilization, airline bankruptcy, market exit, or increased airport capacity) are put back into a "common pot" and then allocated free of charge 50% to new entrants and 50% to existing companies. A company is considered a new entrant if it holds less than 5% of the allocated slots. The restrictive definition of "new entrant" paradoxically leads to slots being allocated to multiple newcomers, with airlines already established but with a low market share finding new slots difficult to obtain. This system favors the entry of small competitors but does little to encourage their growth.
- *The slot exchange rule*: Regulation 95/93 authorizes carriers to exchange or transfer slots between themselves, provided there is no actual sale and the exchange takes place under conditions of transparency. In practice, however, this rule is sometimes circumvented: for example, at London Heathrow airport, American Airlines paid US$60 million in 2015 to acquire a pair of slots allocated to Scandinavian Airlines.

These different rules favor established operators and limit the growth of new entrants, insofar as those who hold slots use them so that they do not go back into the common pot. From one aeronautical season to the next, slots returned to the common pot are usually close to zero. At congested airports, the share of historical slots in total slots is between 80% and 90%, and it even reaches 99% in the case of London Heathrow. However, an airline can always acquire slots by buying out an airline already present at the airport or by applying to take over its slots if it goes bankrupt.

In view of the low mobility of slots between airlines, several reforms of slot regulation have been envisaged, in an effort to encourage the entry of new and more efficient competitors, including:

- Auctioning slots that have fallen into the common pot to ensure that they will be allocated to the airline willing to pay the most. This solution was proposed in the United States in 2009 by the federal regulator for the three New York airports but was rejected by Congress;
- The regular return to the common pot of a certain percentage of slots held by airlines to allow a certain mobility of slots; and
- A reform of the 80/20 rule: to avoid 20% of slots not being used, the 80/20 rule could be tightened by raising the threshold to 90%, for example.

2.2.3 *Flight Safety and Security*

When an airline is allowed to operate at an airport, it must comply with flight safety and security regulations. In terms of flight safety, the challenge is preventing unlawful acts within the airport or during the flight, in particular by making sure that dangerous items such as weapons or explosives are not brought on board. This subject became a major source of concern after the attacks of September 11, 2001. Since then, the regulatory framework applicable in this field has been considerably strengthened in Europe: Regulation 2320/2002 stipulates that all passengers, staff, and baggage must be systematically screened before boarding.

Safety rules were introduced very early on in the air transport industry and cover aircraft design, training and working conditions for flight crews, and accident investigation procedures. For flight crews, rules govern maximum flight times and minimum rest periods, to ensure that the cabin crew and pilots are able to perform their jobs effectively without compromising flight and passenger safety. In Europe, for example, the maximum number of flying hours per year for a pilot is 900.

Although the ICAO has laid down principles for flight safety, each country is free to set its own rules. In Europe, for example, following the completion of the internal air transport market in the 1990s, common, mandatory rules with very high safety standards were adopted. These rules are enforced by the European Commission, the EASA, and the relevant national authorities. In particular, EASA is responsible for inspecting aircrafts when they are at airports in the European Union: this represents more than 6000 inspections per year. If any deficiencies are found, the companies concerned may be placed on a "blacklist" of airlines banned from operating in the European Union for safety reasons. This blacklist is regularly updated and published, so that passengers, ticket vendors, and the relevant authorities are kept informed at all times. In 2024, no fewer than 128 airlines were banned from flying in the European Union, most of them from Africa and Central Asia.

These strict rules on flight safety and security, combined with advances in aircraft technology, explain why the fatal accident rate has fallen sharply over the past

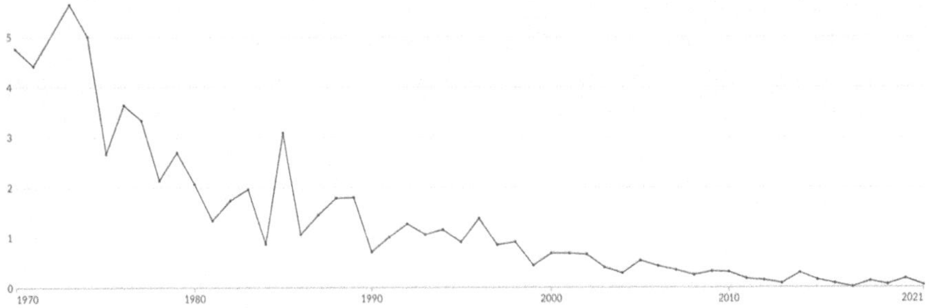

Fig. 2.7 Trends in aviation fatalities (per million passengers). Source: Ourworldindata (2022)

40 years, to the point of stabilizing at a very low level since the 2000s, whatever the indicator used (see Fig. 2.7). For example, the fatal accident rate, defined as the number of accidents per 1 million flights, stands at a level of 0.23 over the 2017–2021 period. On average, this rate has fallen by 8% a year over the past 40 years. But this average masks disparities between regions of the world: in particular, the African continent is characterized by a high accident rate, especially when airlines are not IATA members.

2.2.4 *Passenger Rights*

In addition to safety and security rules, airlines are also subject to passenger rights regulations.

First, when booking a ticket, the customer must be provided with transparent and fair information on the exact content of the service. In Europe, Directive 2005/29 on unfair commercial practices stipulates the following:

- The advertised price must include all unavoidable and foreseeable taxes and charges, such as airport taxes;
- Availability conditions for special offers (e.g., first price) must be clearly indicated;
- Paid options must not be preselected so that the customer subscribes to them voluntarily; and
- General contractual clauses must be clearly written and easily accessible on the website.

In the past, several airlines, notably low-cost carriers, have been penalized for failing to comply with these rules. In France, for example, Ryanair was condemned for having applied a surcharge at the time of ticket payment, depending on the credit card used by the customer. This practice of overcharging is illegal in Europe, unless the company can demonstrate that payment with a particular card entails additional costs.

Similarly, when booking a ticket, the consumer must be able to identify the air carrier that will operate the flight, such as when the flight is a code-share or involves several legs with different airlines. In particular, this system is designed to inform consumers of the risk that an airline authorized to operate from the European Union may sell them a ticket from a blacklisted airline on a journey outside Europe.

Second, if the passenger decides not to show up on the day of the flight, he or she is entitled to claim reimbursement of taxes and fees directly linked to boarding, such as the airport tax and the passenger fee. At the time of the flight, the customer is also protected if the flight is cancelled, delayed, or overbooked. In Europe, Regulation 261/2004 lays down precise rules (see Box 2.2).

Box 2.2 Practical guide in case of flight cancellation, delay, or overbooking

If a flight is canceled, European legislation provides for a minimum ticket refund. In the case of a European flight, special rights apply. The airline must:

- Offer either re-routing on another flight to the final destination under comparable conditions of transport or reimbursement within 7 days for the part not flown but also for the part flown and no longer required;
- If the customer opts for re-routing, the airline must cover all hotel and catering costs until arrival at the final destination.
- Pay lump-sum compensation: €250 for flights under 1500 km, €400 for intra-community flights or flights between 1500 and 3500 km, and €600 for other flights over 3500 km.

If a flight is delayed, except in extraordinary circumstances (e.g., weather conditions, security risks, strikes), passengers who experience a delay of more than 3 h on arrival have the same rights as in the case of cancellation, particularly in terms of compensation. In addition, the airline must provide the passenger with the necessary assistance (e.g., refreshments, catering, telephone, hotel accommodation) as soon as the departure delay of a flight reaches a certain threshold, depending on the distance of the flight.

In the event of overbooking, airlines must first seek volunteers who agree to give up their reservation in exchange for certain services, according to terms to be agreed upon between the passengers concerned and the airline. If the customer does not volunteer and is unable to board, he or she is entitled to compensation (between €250 and €600) depending on the distance of the flight and the delays incurred. The airline must also provide the necessary assistance.

On several occasions, low-cost airlines (Ryanair in particular) have refused to compensate passengers, arguing that they were victims of "extraordinary circumstances" that exempted them from their duty to assist. For example, during the eruption of Iceland's Eyjafjallajökull volcano in April 2010, Ryanair cancelled several flights but did not cover the cost of additional accommodation for stranded passengers, simply refunding the purchase price of their tickets. For this failure, the Irish airline was ordered to pay €3 million in June 2010 by the Italian civil aviation organization, which did not accept the argument of "extraordinary circumstances." In January 2013, the Court of Justice of the European Union confirmed that circumstances such as the closure of part of European airspace following a volcanic eruption did indeed constitute "extraordinary circumstances," but it did not exonerate air carriers from their obligation to take care of passengers.

2.3 Regulating Competitive Behavior

Like any business sector, air transport is subject to competition rules (Combe, 2016). First, anti-competitive behavior by, for example, cartels and abuse of dominant positions are prohibited. Second, mergers and acquisitions (M&A) are subject to prior control by the competition authorities. In the specific case of the European Union, there is also prior control of state aid when it distorts competition within the internal market (Table 2.2).

Table 2.2 The main areas of competition policy

Object	United States	European Union	Air transport business examples
Agreements	Section 1 of the Sherman Act	Article 101 of the TFEU (Treaty on the Functioning of the European Union)	Scandinavian Airlines/ Maersk Air (EU 2001) Air freight cartel (EU 2010) Skyteam Alliance (EU 2015) Alliance One World (EU 2010) Star alliance (EU 2013)
Abuse of dominant position	Section 2 of the Sherman Act	Article 102 of the TFEU	British Airways/Virgin Atlantic (EU 1999) American Airlines (US 2000)
Merger control	Clayton Antitrust Act, section 7	Regulation 139/2004	Air France/KLM (EU 2004) EasyJet/AirBerlin (EU 2017) Ryanair/Aer Lingus (EU 2013)
State aid		Articles 107 and 108	Ryanair/Pau, Nîmes, and Angoulême airports (2014)

2.3.1 From Alliances to Cartels

Horizontal agreements involve competing companies coordinating to achieve certain common objectives. On the one hand, when this coordination does not affect the main parameters of competition (e.g., price, quantity, product quality) and only results in gains for companies or consumers, the agreement is considered lawful. On the other hand, when the agreement concerns strategic variables such as price or quantity, it reduces the autonomy of each company's behavior and therefore risks affecting competition on the market. In such cases, the agreement may be prohibited. An anti-competitive agreement can, however, be "saved" under strict conditions: in particular, companies must demonstrate that the harm to competition is offset by efficiency gains. In Europe, the general principle of prohibiting anti-competitive agreements is enshrined in Article 101 of the TFEU. In the United States, it is covered by Section 1 of the Sherman Act.

In the case of air transport, cooperation between competing airlines is profuse and can take many forms, depending on the degree of cooperation (Fig. 2.8). The first form involves "interline agreements": one airline agrees with another that passengers on a multi-leg flight with both carriers can travel with a single ticket and collect their baggage at the final destination. These agreements, which facilitate passengers' journeys, do not a priori pose any competition problems.

A second case of cooperation between competitors is represented by so-called code-share agreements. A distinction can be made between a horizontal code-share, in which airline B markets a flight operated by airline A under its own brand, and a vertical code-share, in which airline A advertises on its website a flight operated by

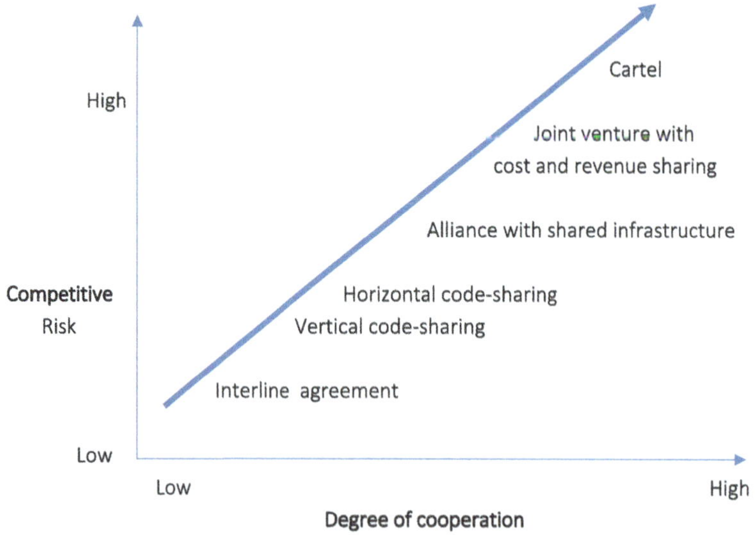

Fig. 2.8 Different degrees of cooperation between airlines. Source: The authors

airline B on a route it does not operate. In 2017, for example, Air France signed a code-share agreement with Singapore Airlines that permitted it to market the Singapore-based airline's flights to Melbourne and Sydney, two routes that Air France does not operate. Vertical agreements help airlines extend the size of their network without serving the destination themselves. Horizontal code-shares, by contrast, enable airlines to market each other's flights on the same route, thereby increasing the frequency of flights offered to customers and boosting aircraft load factors. For example, Air France is code-sharing with Middle East Airlines on the Paris–Beirut route: a Middle East Airlines ticket can be purchased on the Air France website, at a price set by Air France, and vice versa. Code-sharing agreements, whether horizontal or vertical, do not pose any competition problems, as long as each airline retains its own pricing freedom.

A third category involves major alliances, which bring together a multitude of airlines worldwide. There are three main alliances worldwide: Star Alliance, Skyteam, and OneWorld. Each alliance brings together a large number of airlines: Skyteam has no fewer than 20 members. The competitive analysis of these alliances is complex. On the one hand, these alliances are a source of efficiency gains: they enable airlines to pool certain infrastructures (e.g., lounges) and improve the passenger experience, notably by offering more flights. On the other hand, they can reduce competition, by encouraging the exchange of strategic information among members.

A fourth type of alliance is joint ventures, in which several alliance members share revenues, costs, or profits on several routes. This high degree of mutualization is a source of efficiency gains for airlines and customers alike, notably through increased flight frequency. But it can also reduce competition on the route, leading joint venture members to limit capacity or raise ticket prices. In the Skyteam alliance, Air France/KLM, Alitalia, and Delta decided in 2010 to set up a transatlantic joint venture, with the intent to share profits and jointly manage schedules, fares, and capacity on three routes: Amsterdam–New York, Rome–New York, and Paris–New York. Given the high market share of the three airlines combined, the European Commission feared a significant reduction in competition on these three transatlantic routes, resulting in higher ticket prices. To address these concerns, the three alliance members offered a series of commitments, over a 10-year period, designed to enable competitors to develop: these included the surrender of airport slots, agreements enabling competitors to offer tickets on the parties' flights on the three routes, and access to their customer loyalty programs on the three routes.

A final example is when competitors jointly set prices or quantities or share customers, without any efficiency gains. This practice, known as a "cartel," is prohibited and severely punished by the antitrust authorities, since it artificially increases prices. In the case of air transport, the best-known cartel is the air freight cartel, which brought together 11 airlines during the period 1999–2006: its aim was to impose a flat-rate surcharge per kilo on all parcel shipments. Cartel members were fined US$1.7 billion in the United States and €799 million in Europe.

2.3.2 *Abuse of a Dominant Position*

While a company may be in a dominant position due to its intrinsic superiority (e.g., lower costs, better-quality products), it must not abuse this position to drive an equally efficient competitor out of the market. This rule appears in Article 102 of the TFEU and in Section 2 of the Sherman Act. Abuse of a dominant position can take many forms, such as predatory pricing, tied sales, and loyalty discounts.

In particular, predatory pricing involves a dominant company slashing its prices to below its average variable cost, with the intent to force a competitor out of the market. After the competitor has left the market, the dominant firm can then raise its prices to "recoup its losses."

The American Airlines case in the United States (2001) illuminates the difficulty of demonstrating a predatory pricing strategy. Following the entry of low-cost carrier Vanguard on several routes to Dallas in 1996, American Airlines reacted by slashing prices and adding capacity. Vanguard quickly withdrew from the routes, leading American Airlines to raise its fares by 50%. Despite being accused of "predatory pricing," American Airlines was not convicted, as the courts deemed that its actions were simply a competitive response to the entry of a new competitor. Moreover, demonstration of an ability to recoup losses was not sufficiently substantiated.

In Europe, German antitrust authorities investigated a similar practice in 2011 against Lufthansa. Following the entry of low-cost carrier Germania on the Frankfurt–Berlin route, Lufthansa significantly lowered its average ticket price. The German competition authority deemed this predatory pricing, since the average ticket price was below variable costs. For 2 years, it required Lufthansa to charge an average price that was always higher than that of its low-cost competitor, taking into account the cost differential per seat.

2.3.3 *Controlling M&A*

The air transport sector is no exception to the trend toward M&A, particularly in the wake of a crisis. In the United States, after the financial crisis of 2008, a vast market consolidation movement took place, with the merger of the giants Delta Air Lines/Northwest Airlines (2009), United Airlines/Continental Airlines (2011), and American Airlines/US Airways (2013). Such mergers are often guided by considerations of cost savings, in particular to achieve critical mass and synergies between networks. Nevertheless, by removing an independent competitor from the market (while possibly retaining the acquired airline's brand), M&A can reduce competition in the market and lead to higher ticket prices. The borderline case is that of a merger between two airlines that would be the only ones present on the market: the operation would de facto result in a monopoly.

To prevent competition from being reduced too much, merger projects in most countries are subject to compulsory prior control, as soon as certain sales thresholds are crossed. In Europe, merger control rules are set out in Regulation 139/2004; in the United States, they are set out in Section 7 of the Clayton Antitrust Act (1914). It should be noted that this control applies to all companies operating within an economic area, even if they are owned by third countries. For example, the merger between US Airways and American Airlines in 2013 was subject to control not only by the US authorities but also by the European Commission, on the grounds that both companies operate in Europe.

To assess the impact of a merger on competition, the first step is to define the "relevant market" in which the merging parties operate. In the case of air transport, markets are usually defined on a route-by-route basis, according to a point-of-origin/point-of-destination approach (known as the "O&D approach"). In other words, the market is defined as a transport service between two cities or two airports (e.g., the Paris Orly–Milan Malpensa route). Other indices are also taken into account, such as the types of passengers carried (e.g., tourists, business customers), the role of intermodal competition (e.g., the presence of a high-speed train line), the substitutability between airports (e.g., between London Heathrow and Gatwick), and the substitutability between direct and connecting flights.

After the various markets are defined, the second step is to analyze the evolution of the merging companies' market shares on each of the relevant markets: if post-merger market shares are high, a risk is that the operation will have a negative impact on competition. A scenario of harm to competition is then constructed, and three cases can be distinguished:

1. When both airlines operate between the same cities, the risk is that ticket prices will rise on the routes affected.
2. When both airlines use the same airports as their base, the risk is that new entrants will be denied access to slots.
3. When one of the companies supplies feeder traffic and the other uses feeder traffic, the risk is of feeder traffic being locked in.

Other factors are also taken into account to assess the likely impact of the merger on competition, such as the degree of competitive proximity between the airlines. If they target the same type of customer (e.g., business people), the risk of ticket price rises is greater. Similarly, the possibility of a competitor entering the market is taken into account. For example, at a congested airport, a new airline is unlikely to counteract the price rise, given a lack of available slots.

In the third stage, any efficiency gains from the merger are analyzed. A merger can reduce production costs, for example, by making better use of economies of scale. However, such efficiency gains are rarely taken into account in practice, given the difficulty of quantifying them.

If the proposed merger poses a threat to competition, its completion may be conditional on the implementation of "remedies." A common structural remedy in the air transport sector is to cede slots to a competitor. In 2004, for example, the European Commission authorized the Air France/KLM merger, but it required the divestment of 94 slots in view of identified competition problems on several routes, such as Amsterdam–Paris. This commitment was accompanied by a measure requiring Air France and KLM not to increase their flight capacity ("frequency freeze") on the affected routes, to give new entrants the chance to establish themselves as credible competitors.

In extreme cases, a merger may even be prohibited. In Europe, for example, the European Commission blocked Ryanair's takeover of Irish airline Aer Lingus in 2013. This takeover would have led to the merger of the two main airlines operating in Ireland, with a combined market share of 87% for short-haul flights from Dublin. The European Commission found that the merger would have harmed consumers by creating a dominant position in 46 routes. No sufficient remedies were identified to restore competition.

2.3.4 *State Aid Control*

In Europe, a general principle, codified in Article 107 of the TFEU, is that any state aid that distorts competition is prohibited. The goal is to prevent a company from gaining an unfair advantage over its competitors on the grounds that it benefits from public support. However, if a state wishes to grant aid to a company, it must first notify the European Commission.

There is, however, a system of exemptions from the obligation of prior notification, known as "block exemptions": here, some types of aid are automatically authorized, provided they meet certain conditions. In the case of air transport, for example, some public aid to airports or airlines can be "exempted."

For example, public authorities can temporarily support the development of regional airports (fewer than 3 million passengers per year), with the aim to improve a region's accessibility. Aid granted to regional airports must meet several conditions: it must correspond to a real transport need, it must be necessary to guarantee the accessibility of a region, and it must be proportionate to the size of the airport.

Public subsidies for starting up a new route may also be authorized, provided they are limited in time. In practice, such aid is often granted to low-cost airlines, such as Ryanair, that set up in small airports and open new routes. If state aid has been paid illegally, the European Commission can force it to be repaid. Since the 2000s, Europe has seen an abundance of litigation regarding the illegality of state aid, mainly targeting low-cost airlines. In 2014, for example, Ryanair and Transavia had to repay almost €10 million for having received illegal state aid from the airports in Angoulême, Nîmes, and Pau.

In response to the COVID-19 crisis, the European Commission considerably relaxed the rules on state aid, authorizing direct aid in the form of guaranteed loans and targeted aid for the recapitalization of companies experiencing difficulty due to the pandemic. Such aid must comply with the principles of necessity and proportionality: it must not exceed the minimum necessary to guarantee the viability of the aided company. This emergency aid has particularly affected the airline industry, whose traffic fell by more than 90% during the periods of lockdown. For example, the European Commission approved Germany's plan to contribute €6 billion to the recapitalization of Lufthansa. But this decision came with strict measures to limit distortions of competition. In particular, Lufthansa agreed to make available slots and additional assets at its Frankfurt and Munich hub airports, where the airline has significant market power. These measures enable a viable entry or expansion of activities by other airlines at these airports to the benefit of consumers and effective competition.

References

Airports Council International. (2024). *Annual world airport traffic*. https://aci.aero/2024/07/16/top-20-busiest-airports-in-the-world-confirmed-by-aci-world/

Combe, E. (2016). *La politique de la concurrence*. La Découverte, collection Repères (3rd ed.).

IATA. (2022). *Outsized market power in parts of the aviation value chain*. IATA Economics' Chart of the Week.

ICAO. (2013). 50th Conference of Directors General of Civil Aviation Asia and Pacific Regions Economic development of air transport Current Challenges, 42 p.

Moore, N. Y., Grammich, C. A., DaVanzo, J., Held, B., Coombs, J., & Mele, J. D. (2008). Enhancing small-business opportunities in the DoD, RAND Corporation Report. https://apps.dtic.mil/sti/tr/pdf/ADA489545.pdf

Morrison, J., Sgouridis, S., & Hansman, R. (2011). *Game theory analysis if aircraft manufacturer innovation strategies in the face of increasing airline fuel costs*. Report No. ICAT-2011-4, MIT International Center for Air Transportation.

Our World in Data. (2022). *Global aviation fatalities per million passengers*.

Chapter 3
The Airline Business Model

An airline's main function is to "produce" flights whose seats will be sold to passengers (passenger transport) or to produce capacity for customers wishing to transport goods (freight or cargo transport). To carry out this activity, the airline must use inputs, capital (e.g., an aircraft), and labor (e.g., pilots, cabin crew). This production can give rise to different costs.

In the first part of this chapter, we explain the nature of these costs, which are fixed or variable. We also show that airlines perform very differently in terms of unit production costs, partly as a result of their business model.

In the second part, we analyze revenues and the determinants of the ticket price, emphasizing the key role of dynamic pricing, which causes the price of a ticket on the same flight to evolve over time. We also show that airlines perform quite differently in their ability to generate revenues.

In the third part, we compare revenues with costs, to assess whether a company is profitable or not. We highlight the differences in profitability between companies, emphasizing the key role of consistency between the level of costs and revenues.

3.1 Airline Costs

When a passenger airline produces flights, the quantity produced is measured in available seat–kilometers (ASK). This is the number of seats available multiplied by the distance covered by the seat during the flight (measured in kilometers). The length of the flight must be taken into account when assessing the "quantity produced." For example, let's assume that airline A carries 180 passengers every day on a 500 km flight, while airline B, with the same number of passengers, travels 1000 km. It would be wrong to consider that both airlines produce the same quantity, since airline B travels twice as far each day. In our example, airline B produces 180 × 1000 = 180,000 ASK, while airline A produces 90,000 ASK.

P. Chiambaretto, E. Combe, *Introduction to Air Transport*, SpringerBriefs in Business, https://doi.org/10.1007/978-3-031-99936-9_3

To produce a certain quantity of ASK, an airline must bear different costs, broken down into fixed costs, which do not vary with quantities, and variable costs, which depend on the quantity produced. The total cost of production for an airline carrying passengers can therefore be written as

$$Total\ cost = A + cQ \quad with\, c > 0,$$

where A is the fixed cost, c is the variable cost, and Q is the quantity, measured in ASK.

3.1.1 Fixed and Variable Airline Costs

Fixed costs are all costs that do not vary with the quantity produced. So, even if an airline doesn't fly, as was the case during the COVID-19 crisis, it must still bear all fixed costs. The higher the fixed costs are in relation to variable costs, the more difficult it is for an airline to temporarily suspend flights. On average, an airline's fixed costs can represent up to 50% of its total costs (Fig. 3.1).

The breakdown between fixed and variable costs depends on the business model chosen: low-cost airlines tend to have a higher proportion of variable costs than traditional carriers, which enables them to be more flexible (and therefore incur fewer losses) in case of a negative shock. Fuel, for example, which is a variable cost, represents the first cost item for a company like Ryanair (more than 40%), whereas it accounts for only 20% for an incumbent such as Air France or British Airways. Conversely, staff costs, which are largely fixed, account for 30% of costs at a traditional airline like Lufthansa, compared with just 13% at Ryanair.

The breakdown between fixed and variable costs also depends on the size of the company: a small airline will tend to outsource many functions to service providers, paying for them only when used. Conversely, large airlines internalize many

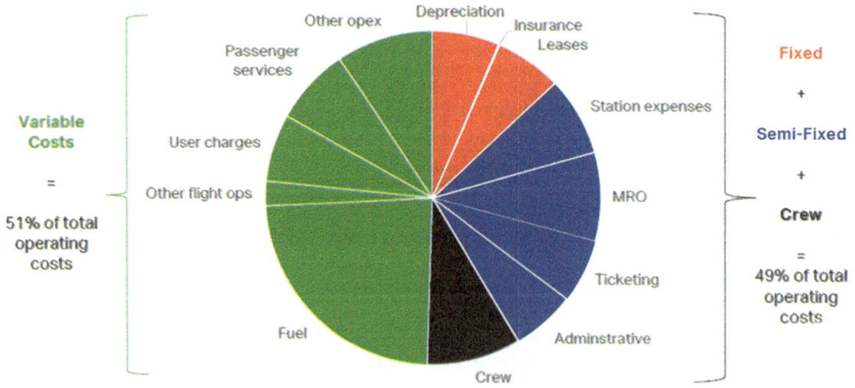

Fig. 3.1 Fixed and variable airline costs. Source: IATA (2020)

functions, such as aircraft maintenance and ground handling, which generates higher fixed costs.

The distinction between fixed and variable costs also depends on the time horizon chosen. In the short run, the majority of costs are mostly fixed. For example, an airline that doesn't fly for several weeks must nevertheless continue to pay its employees basic wages, as well as aircraft rental. Taking a longer-term view, the company can adjust its size, either upward or downward: if economic conditions are poor, it may decide to let some of its employees go or terminate an aircraft lease. Conversely, in a booming economy, it can increase the number of aircrafts and recruit new flight crews.

An airline incurs the following main fixed costs:

- *The cost of purchasing or leasing the aircraft* ("depreciation and lease"): if the aircraft is owned by the company, depreciation must be taken into account so that the company can buy it back when it becomes obsolete. If the company purchased the aircraft on credit, it will have to repay a certain amount of the loan every month, even if it doesn't use the aircraft. Similarly, a company can lease an aircraft, including its commercial and technical crew; this case is known as an ACMI (aircraft, crew, maintenance, and insurance) *wet* lease.
- *Costs associated with owning an aircraft*: these include insurance and airport parking fees ("station expenses").
- *Part of the aircraft's maintenance, repair and overhaul* ("MRO") *costs*: even if the aircraft is not flying, the company still must undertake regular check-ups, as was the case during the COVID-19 crisis. Major maintenance visits are also mandatory at regular intervals.
- *Part of the remuneration of flight crews*: for most airlines, flight crews, particular pilots and cabin crew, have a salaried status. Part of their remuneration is therefore independent of whether they fly and constitutes a fixed cost. It should be noted, however, that remuneration levels can vary widely between airlines. In particular, some low-cost airlines, such as Ryanair, offer lower total and hourly remuneration than incumbent airlines. Moreover, airlines such as Buzz, a Ryanair subsidiary, sometimes use self-employed flight crews during the high season: this status transforms the cost of labor into a variable cost, as pilots and cabin crew are only paid when they fly.
- *Costs associated with owning airport assets*: these include, for example, check-in counters, lounges, and ramp personnel.
- *Distribution fixed costs.*
- *Administrative costs*: these correspond to all the cross-functional support functions that make air transport possible. These may include, for example, the cost of head office, sales agencies or airport ground services, the salaries of human resources, marketing, IT, and flight planning personnel.

Regarding variable costs, an airline essentially has five main costs:

- *The cost of fuel*: this cost is more or less the same in absolute terms for all airlines, except when they have pre-purchased volumes of oil at a certain price (a practice known as "hedging"). The older the aircraft and its engines, the higher is the cost of fuel. Each new generation of engines brings efficiency gains in fuel consumption of around 15%.

- Ground handling *costs*: these include loading/unloading the aircraft's hold and preparing meals served on board ("catering").
- *Variable compensation for flight crews*: such compensation can be very high for low-cost airlines, particularly for cabin crew, who are partly remunerated by commissions on on-board sales.
- *Part of the maintenance costs directly linked to aircraft use*: as soon as an aircraft begins to fly, it undergoes regular inspections. An aircraft undergoes a quick daily inspection, then a light inspection (depending on the number of flight hours or landing and takeoff cycles), and finally a heavy inspection.
- *Commissions linked to ticket distribution:* ticket sales may entail the payment of commissions to travel agencies or GDSs. These distribution costs are lower when the company decides to sell tickets directly, such as via its own website.
- *Airport taxes and charges linked to air travel*: some of these taxes and charges are only paid if the aircraft actually flies. Civil aviation or airport taxes are levied on each passenger or flight and are included in the ticket price. The amount of these taxes and charges can vary depending on the size of the airfield, the route taken by the aircraft, or the weight of the aircraft. Similarly, every aircraft that lands must pay a fee, the amount of which depends on the airport, the infrastructure used, and the weight of the aircraft.

3.1.2 Significant Differences in Unit Costs Between Airlines

After we have listed all variable and fixed costs, we can add them together to obtain the total cost. We can then calculate the unit cost by dividing the total cost by the quantities produced (see Box 3.1). As production quantities are measured in ASK in air transport, the unit cost corresponds to the CASK (cost per available seat–kilometers).

$$CASK = \frac{Total\ cost}{Quantity} = \frac{Fixed\ costs + variable\ costs}{ASK}.$$

This indicator measures the cost of transporting a seat 1 km. Because the CASK includes fixed costs such as the aircraft, it necessarily decreases with the average distance flown. Indeed, the longer the flights, the more kilometers the aircraft covers in a day, and the more fixed costs are spread over a higher number of ASK.

Box 3.1 An example of CASK

Airline A makes a daily flight of 800 km in a 180-seat aircraft. It rents an aircraft with crew, paying a daily rental of €10,000. Each occupied seat costs the airline €40 in fuel and taxes.

Its total cost for a flight is therefore equal to its daily fixed cost and its variable cost:

$$\text{Total cost} = 10{,}0000 + (0.9 \times 180) \times 40 = €16{,}480.$$

Its daily ASK on the route are equal to:

$$\text{ASK} = 180 \times 800 = 144{,}000$$

Its CASK is therefore equal to

$$CASK = \frac{16{,}480}{144{,}000} = €0.11$$

This means that, on average, on this route, transporting a seat over 1 km costs 11 cents.

Given the presence of fixed costs, the CASK tends to decrease with flight distance, as Fig. 3.2 shows. For CASK comparisons between airlines, we need to consider equivalent distances, distinguishing between medium-haul and long-haul, for example.

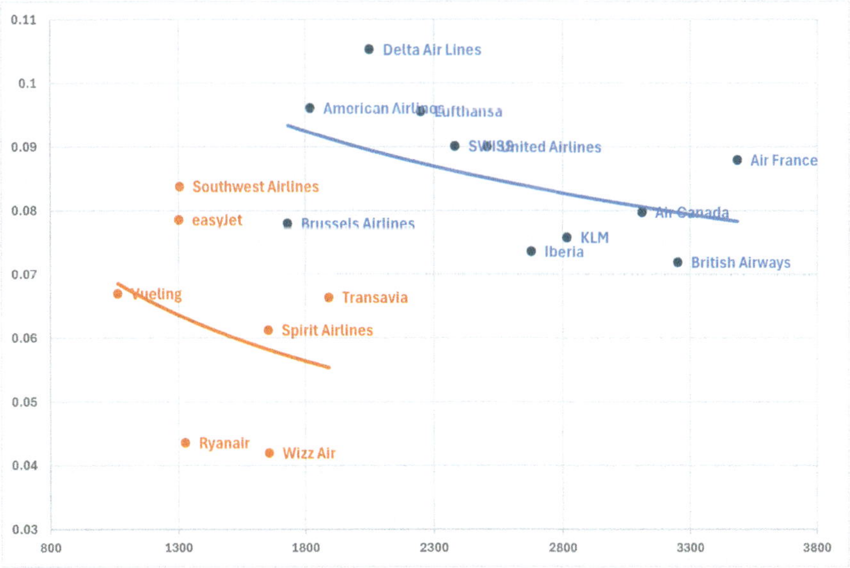

Fig. 3.2 CASK level and flight distance. Source: Kuljanin and Kalic (2016)

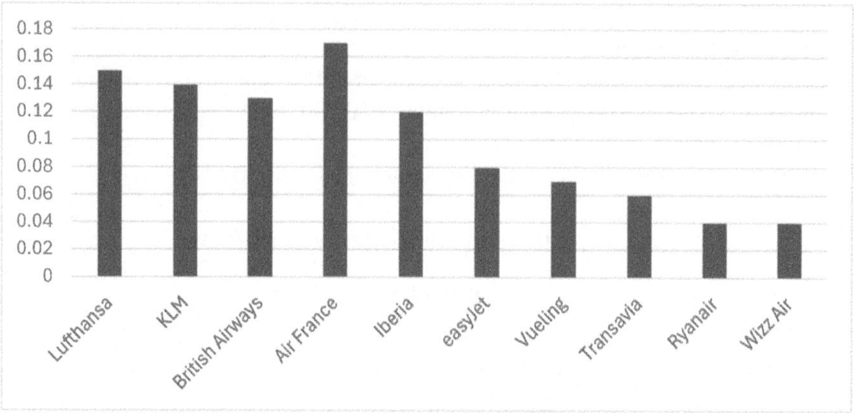

Fig. 3.3 Main European airlines' CASKs for intra-European flights (2023). Source: The authors, based on RDC Apex 2024

In Fig. 3.3, we compare the CASKs of the main European airlines only for their intra-European flights. We show that CASK varies widely between European airlines on short- and medium-haul flights alone:

- The first group includes traditional airlines such as Air France and Lufthansa, with a CASK of between 12 and 17 cents.
- The second group is made up of *low-cost* airlines such as EasyJet, Transavia, or Vueling, whose CASKs are between 6 and 8 cents, that is, 40% lower than those of a traditional airline.
- The third group includes *low-cost* carriers such as Wizz Air and Ryanair (sometimes referred to as ultra-low-cost carriers), which offer very low CASKs of around 4 cents, or 80% less than those of an incumbent carrier on a medium-haul flight.

It should be noted that these differences in CASK also occur in the United States, but to a lesser extent: in 2019, *low-cost* airlines such as Spirit or Frontier posted CASKs of around 7 cents, compared with 10 cents for Southwest Airlines and 12 cents for the incumbents, such as Delta and American.

What causes these CASK differences between incumbents and low-cost carriers? We can conduct a simulation to break down the cost gap, taking the example of a low-cost airline whose production cost is 33% lower than that of an incumbent airline, corresponding to a so-called middle-cost airline (Fig. 3.4). The main lesson is that the total cost differential results from the addition of several cost reductions. Figure 3.4 shows that the first two levers, which together account for half the cost differential, are the greater productivity of pilots and cabin crews (8-point difference; i.e., 24%) and fleet and maintenance management (8-point difference). Next, in descending order, we find reductions in distribution costs (5 points), support functions (4 points), kerosene expenditure linked to the use of recent aircraft (3

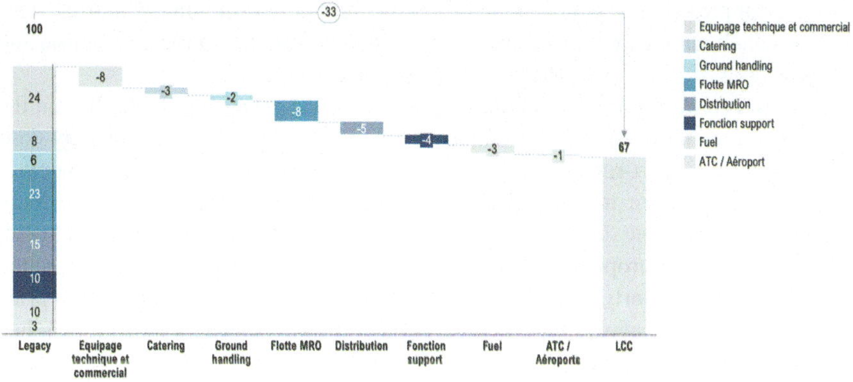

Fig. 3.4 Origin of cost differentials between *low-cost* and traditional airlines (2019). Source: Roland Berger (2022)

points), supply costs (3 points), ground handling costs (2 points), and, finally, airport taxes (1 point).

3.2 Airline Revenues

An airline's income (also known as "revenues") comes mainly from the sale of airline tickets, but it also comes from the sale of paying options (known as "ancillary revenues"). Thus, an airline's total revenue corresponds to the number of tickets and options sold multiplied by their various prices:

$$Total\ revenue = Airline\ tickets\ sales + ancillary\ revenues.$$

Total revenue will depend on both the average price of a ticket ("yield") and the quantity of tickets sold, which in turn depends on aircraft load and seat capacity (measured in ASK).

3.2.1 Ticket Prices and the Role of Dynamic Pricing

When setting ticket prices, airlines must take several structural factors into account:

- *Unit production cost*: in case of a cost shock, airlines will increase their ticket prices. For example, the sharp rise in ticket prices in Europe in the summer of 2022 was due in part to the soaring price of oil: while it represented 15% of total costs for a traditional carrier, its weight almost doubled to 29%. Airline taxes also have an impact on production costs and, thus, on ticket prices. In July 2006, for example, a tax was introduced in France to help developing countries. This tax, which ranges from an additional €1 to €40 depending on the destination and class booked, was fully passed on to ticket prices.

- *Anticipated demand*: when demand is strong, ticket prices will be higher on the same route. This impact of demand on price is reinforced by the capacity constraint in the short run: for example, an aircraft with 180 seats cannot increase seat capacity even if demand becomes strong. Price then becomes the main adjustment variable. During the summer season, for example, many people travel to the South of Europe for their vacations, which means higher prices than in the low season. Similarly, ticket prices depend on the sensitivity of demand to price (known as "price elasticity"): this means that if more people want to travel during a certain time, the price will be higher. For example, on the Barcelona–Madrid route, business travelers often want to leave early for a 1-day round trip: such tickets are therefore more expensive in the early morning than in the late morning. Even with low production costs, selling at a high price is rational for a company when demand is strong or price-inelastic. It is not surprising that a *low-cost* company charges high prices in the high season or for the most attractive time slots.
- *The intensity of competition on the line*: as a general rule, the greater the number of airlines, the lower are the prices, as each airline runs the risk that customers will turn to the competitor. Conversely, when a company finds itself in a monopoly position on a route, it charges a monopoly price, which is higher than a competitive price, even if its production costs are low. Thus, when a company goes on strike, its competitor will raise its prices. For example, during the Air France strike in September 2014, EasyJet adjusted its prices upward on routes like Paris–Toulouse. However, monopoly power is limited by the price sensitivity of demand: the higher the price elasticity, the less the airline will be able to raise its prices.

In practice, an airline will not apply a single ticket price to a flight but a multiplicity of prices. This multiplicity of prices can be understood from both a static and dynamic standpoint.

From a static standpoint (i.e., at a given moment in time), two seats on the same aircraft and in the same class of travel (e.g., economy class) can be sold at different prices. These price differences (known as "fare discrimination") can be explained by airlines using signals to guess information about customers and how much they are willing to pay. For example, a passenger who books a round-trip ticket between London and Rome on the same day on the internet is more likely to be a business passenger: he or she is likely to be traveling to Rome for a meeting rather than for sightseeing. The price of the ticket will therefore be more expensive than if the outward and return journeys are booked several days (e.g., a weekend) apart. Similarly, on a route between Hamburg and Frankfurt, some passengers will stop off in Frankfurt, while others will continue on to, for example, New York or Tokyo. By booking a ticket that stops in Frankfurt, the passengers are "taking the seats" of other passengers who could be flying on a connecting flight following this flight. As the opportunity cost is high for the airline, it will "punish" the passengers who stop in Frankfurt (and take the seats of passengers who were continuing on) by setting a higher price.

From a dynamic standpoint, airlines have been pioneers in the development and use of "dynamic" pricing techniques (known as "yield management" or "revenue management"). *Yield management* involves adjusting ticket prices in real time, on the same flight and for the same class of travel, in such a way as to maximize the total revenue generated by the flight. The art of *yield management* lies in setting a starting price on the day the flight is opened to bookings and "steering" its evolution over time, right up to the day of the flight:

- If the price increases too quickly, the aircraft may not be full on the day of take-off, which will limit total revenue (quantity effect).
- If the price is too low when reservations open, the flight will be fully booked on the day of departure, but the airline will not have been able to sell tickets at a high price (price effect).

Dynamic pricing involves creating different fares for the same flight in advance. The total capacity of an aircraft (in seats) is therefore subdivided into several reservation classes (each assigned a letter) that correspond to different fares and conditions (e.g., refundable or non-refundable ticket, exchangeable or non-exchangeable ticket). These different fares are displayed over time, depending on the reservation date in relation to the departure date. For example, a customer who books a ticket when a flight opens (6 months or 1 year in advance) will pay a low price, but the ticket will likely not be refundable or exchangeable. This type of ticket corresponds more to the profile of tourists than business customers: they know their vacation dates in advance and therefore can commit themselves with a high degree of certainty. Many are also price-sensitive: beyond a certain psychological price, they may give up traveling by air and turn to other modes of transport or other less expensive destinations. As the flight's departure date draws near and/or the aircraft fills up almost to capacity, the most advantageous fare classes (in terms of price) will be closed, and the price of the ticket will rise. Ticket prices peak on the day before or the day of departure: if someone books on these days, the reason is likely because they weren't able to anticipate their trip, they're traveling for business reasons, or they are dealing with a major constraint. They will therefore accept the high ticket price, as they are not very price-elastic. Moreover, even if the plane isn't full the day before takeoff, many airlines will not lower the price, so that customers don't get into the habit of waiting until the last minute to book their tickets.

As a general rule, therefore, ticket prices for the same flight increase almost continuously, from 3 months before the flight to the day of departure (Fig. 3.5). The amplitude of the price increase can be quite steep: in the case of Ryanair, for example, the price of a ticket can reach €180 on the day of departure, or six times the price observed 3 months before (€30).

In addition to the difference between the reservation date and the flight date, dynamic pricing takes into account several factors, such as the following:

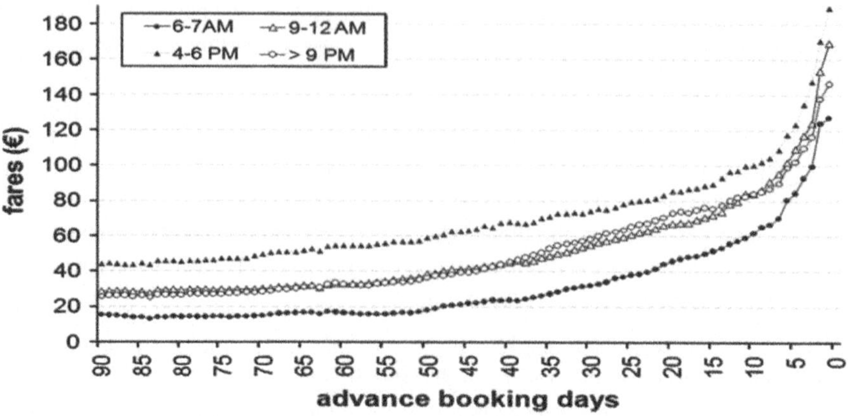

Fig. 3.5 Evolution of the price of a Ryanair ticket by booking date. Source: Malighetti et al. (2009)

- *Season, day, and time of flight*: a flight in high season, on a day of high demand (e.g., a vacation weekend), or in an attractive time slot (e.g., the morning for a medium-haul flight) will be sold at a higher price, and
- *Foreseeable or unforeseeable events*: for example, a sporting event in a capital city (demand factor) or a strike by competitors (competition factor) will mechanically increase ticket prices.

With the development of online reservations, dynamic pricing could evolve into truly personalized pricing. Indeed, with the increase in the collection of individual data, airlines will be able to know precisely customers' maximum willingness to pay and will be able to offer them different prices (Combe, 2019). The number of prices on a flight will then become equal to the number of seats sold on that flight.

3.2.2 The Role of Ancillary Revenues

Ancillary revenues include all airline revenues not directly generated by the sale of an airline ticket. These include revenues generated by the sale of options, such as additional checked baggage, meals or beverages on board, the selection of particular seats in the aircraft, access to in-flight Wi-Fi, and so on.

These ancillary revenues are the result of the *unbundling* of the "all-inclusive" air ticket into a set of sub-products: the one-way ticket and the various options. This breakdown was initiated by low-cost airlines as a way of reducing ticket costs by offering passengers the option of paying only for what they use.

Ancillary services can be distinguished according to the revenue–cost ratio they generate. On the one hand, some services generate additional revenue but also increase costs. This is the case, for example, with in-flight food. On the other hand, some ancillary services generate a "pure margin"; that is, they are billed to the

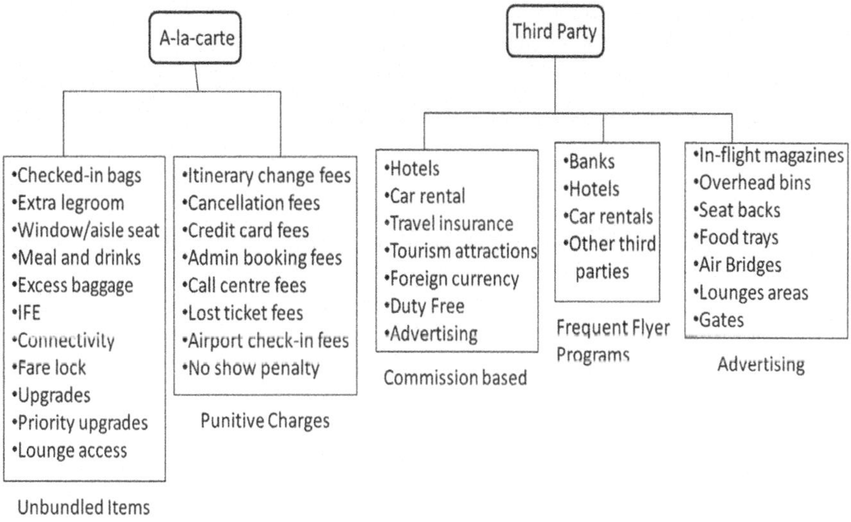

Fig. 3.6 A classification of ancillary revenues. Source: Warnock-Smith et al. (2015)

passengers who use them, without generating additional costs for the airline. This is the case, for example, with payment for priority boarding or seat selection. These options do not create additional costs, but they can be quite profitable. Ancillary revenues can also be classified according to whether they are offered directly by the airline or by a third party (see Fig. 3.6).

These ancillary revenues can account for more than 50% of the total revenues of some low-cost airlines in the United States (e.g., Spirit, Frontier) and up to 40% of the total revenues of European low-cost airlines (e.g., Ryanair). Initially introduced by low-cost airlines, these ancillary services are now increasingly being offered by traditional airlines. Indeed, to make their tickets more attractive in the face of low-cost competition, traditional airlines have also begun breaking down their tickets and offering option sales.

3.2.3 *Sharp Differences in Unit Revenues Between Companies*

By multiplying the prices of the various tickets (and paying options) by the corresponding quantities, we obtain an airline's total revenue. To determine the average revenue, we can divide the total revenue by the quantities offered:

$$\text{Average revenue} = \frac{\text{Total revenue}}{\text{Quantity}}.$$

As we have shown, in the case of passenger air transport, the usual measure of quantity is the ASK (available seat–kilometers), or the number of seats offered multiplied by the distance of the flight. Dividing a company's total revenue by the number of ASKs gives the average revenue per available seat–kilometer (RASK) (see Box 3.2 for details on revenue metrics):

$$RASK = \frac{Total\ revenue}{ASK}$$

Box 3.2 RASK, ASK, RPK, yield, and load factor: understanding revenue metrics

Several indicators in the air transport industry measure a company's ability to generate revenue. In addition to RASK and ASK, RPK (revenue per seat–kilometer), yield, and load factor are commonly used.

RPK measures the number of seat–kilometers occupied on a given flight. It therefore takes into account whether the aircraft is full or not.

The ratio of RPK to ASK therefore measures the aircraft's load factor.

If we divide the total revenue by the number of seat–kilometers occupied, we obtain the average price at which a seat has been sold over 1 km: this is the yield.

The RASK can also be rewritten as

$$RASK = \frac{Total\ revenue}{ASK}$$

$$\Leftrightarrow RASK = \frac{Total\ revenue}{RPK} \times \frac{RPK}{ASK}$$

$$\Leftrightarrow RASK = Unit\ revenue \times load\ factor.$$

The RASK is therefore equal to the unit revenue (per seat and per kilometer) multiplied by the aircraft's load factor.

The numerical example shown in Box 2.1 illustrates these different concepts. An airline operates a daily flight with a capacity of 180 seats over 800 km. Each day, it carries 162 passengers, each of whom has paid €100. Its total revenue is therefore 162 × 100 = €16,200. The flight generated is: (180 × 800) = 144,000 ASK. The RPK on this flight is: (162 × 800) = 129,600. This gives the aircraft's load factor of (129,600/144,000) = 90%. Unit revenue is: 16,200/129,600 = €0.125 per seat occupied over 1 km, or just over 12 cents.

The RASK is therefore equal to: (0.125 × 0.9) = €0.1125.

When comparing RASKs between airlines, it is necessary, as with CASKs, to take flight distance into account: the longer the flight, the lower the RASK will be, since revenue is not proportional to distance. We therefore need to "normalize" RASKs over the same distance to make comparisons between airlines.

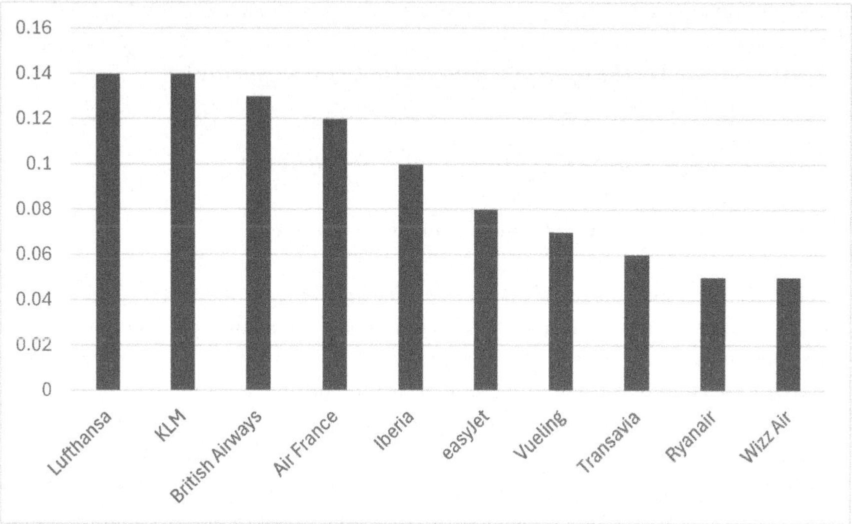

Fig. 3.7 European airlines' RASKs for intra-European flights (2023). Source: The authors, based on RDC Apex 2024

In Fig. 3.7, we compare the RASKs of the main European airlines for intra-European flights. In 2023, RASK levels were heterogeneous, so we can again classify airlines into three groups:

- The first group includes traditional airlines such as Lufthansa, KLM, Air France, and British Airways with RASKs higher than 10 cents.
- The second group is made up of historic or *low-cost* airlines such as EasyJet, Transavia, or Vueling, whose RASKs are between 6 and 8 cents.
- The third group includes only *ultra-low-cost carriers* such as Ryanair and Wizz Air with RASKs around 4 cents.

A similar situation can be found in the United States, with ultra-low-cost airlines such as Frontier and Spirit posting RASKs of less than 9 cents per kilometer; low-cost airlines such as Southwest and JetBlue posting RASKs 30% higher, at around 12 cents; and incumbent airlines such as Delta, United, and American posting RASKs of between 13 and 15 cents.

3.3 Airline Profitability

If we know an airline's total revenues and costs, we can assess its profitability, or its ability to make a profit, as follows:

$$\Pi = Total\ revenue - total\ cost.$$

Since total revenues and costs depend on quantities, we can write total profit as

$$\Pi = (Price \times Quantity) - (Unit\ cost \times quantity)$$

$$\Leftrightarrow \Pi = (Price - Unit\ cost) \times quantity$$

$$\Leftrightarrow \Pi = (Unit\ margin) \times quantity.$$

A company therefore makes a profit when its unit margin is positive and when it sells a non-zero quantity of tickets. A company's total profit thus depends on both its margin and its size: a company may make a high margin but sell very few products (particularly when it's in a niche market), resulting in a low total profit; conversely, a company may make a low margin but sell large volumes, resulting in a high total profit.

In air transport, unit revenue (per ASK) is represented by the RASK, and unit cost (per ASK) corresponds to the CASK. An airline makes a positive margin (equal to RASK – CASK) and a profit when its RASK exceeds its CASK. That is:

$$\Pi = (RASK - CASK) \times quantity.$$

An airline's profitability depends not so much on its level of CASK or RASK as on the comparison between the two:

- A company can have a high level of RASK and still experience a loss if its RASK is lower than its CASK. This is the case for many European airlines on medium-haul routes, such as British Airways and Lufthansa.
- A company can have a low level of RASK and still make a profit if its CASK is lower than its RASK. This is the case with ultra-low-cost airlines such as Ryanair and Wizz Air.
- An airline can have a high CASK level and still be profitable if it has a higher RASK level. This is the case of middle-cost airlines such as EasyJet.

In the United States, airlines also show very different margin levels, ranging from 2 cents to 3.4 cents in 2016. The discrepancy is also striking when the margin is related to sales, given the margin rate: while it reaches almost 24% for low-cost carrier Southwest, it's just 1.9% for United. Generally speaking, low-cost carriers, with the exception of Frontier, have higher margins than incumbents. A similar case occurs in Europe (Chiambaretto & Combe, 2023).

Margin alone does not determine an airline's profit. The "size" effect (i.e., the number of seats sold) also plays an important role. Figure 3.8, which focuses on intra-European flights in 2019, crosses the dimensions "size" and "margin per passenger" for four major airline categories:

- Small airlines with low unit margins, such as Brussels Airlines or Austrian (Group A; shown in white);
- Large airlines with low unit margins, such as Air France and Lufthansa (Group B; shown in light gray);

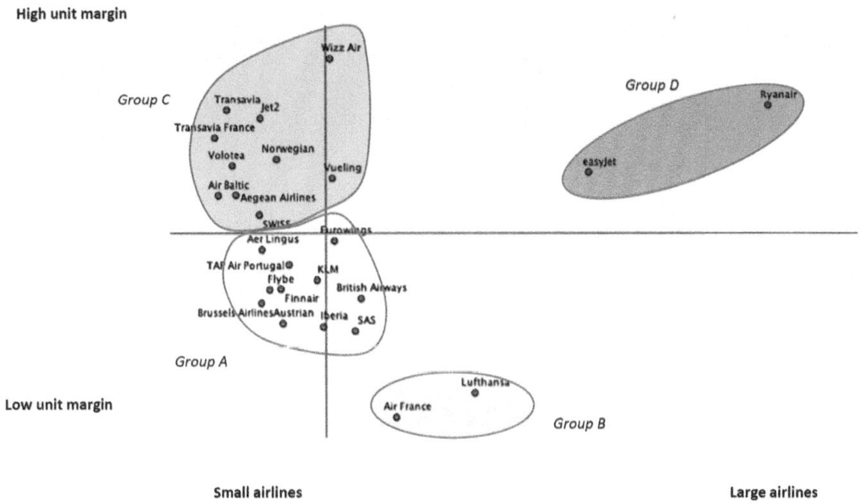

Fig. 3.8 European airline groups by size and unit margin (medium-haul, 2019). Source: Adapted from Chiambaretto and Combe (2023)

- Small, high-margin airlines such as Transavia and Wizz Air (Group C; shown in gray); and
- Large, high-margin airlines such as Ryanair and EasyJet (Group D; shown in dark gray).

This typology reveals that there is no clear correlation between airline size and profitability. This race to be the "largest" airline is not always relevant and motivates us to reflect on the strategies airlines implement in Chap. 4.

References

Chiambaretto, P., & Combe, E. (2023). Business model hybridization but heterogeneous economic performance: Insights from low-cost and legacy carriers in Europe. *Transport Policy, 136*, 83–97.

Combe, E. (2019). *Le low cost*. La Découverte, collection Repères (2nd ed.).

IATA. (2020, March 31). *COVID 19 Cash burn analysis*.

Kuljanin, J., & Kalic, M. (2016). The uprise of the middle east carriers: Emirates' path towards success. *Symorg Conference*, 1405–1412.

Malighetti, P., Paleari, S., & Redondi, R. (2009). Pricing strategies of low-cost airlines: The Ryanair case study. *Journal of Air Transport Management, 15*(4), 195–203.

Roland Berger. (2022). *Future of long distance mobility: Study extract*.

Warnock-Smith, D., O'Connell, J., & Maleki, M. (2015). *An examination of ongoing trends in airline ancillary revenues*. The 19th Air Transport Research Society (ATRS) World Conference, Singapore.

Chapter 4
Competition in the Air Transport Industry

To benefit from the growth in air traffic, airlines are deploying a variety of strategies, depending on the geographic markets or customer groups they are targeting. These strategies echo those Michael Porter identified in his pioneering work *Competitive Advantage* (1985): the cost leadership strategy, the differentiation strategy, and the niche strategy.

In this chapter, we first focus on the cost leadership strategy, as it is widely used on the short- and medium-haul market (up to three or four flight hours), with the growing role of the low-cost model. In the second part, we show that airlines are adopting two other strategic approaches in the long-haul market (over 4-h flight time): some airlines are playing the differentiation card by betting on an upscale offer, while others are applying low-cost recipes. Finally, in the third section, we analyze a niche strategy some airlines are implementing—namely, offering "100% business" flights.

4.1 Short- and Medium-Haul: The Low-Cost Revolution

In the early 1970s, a new business model was born in the United States: the low-cost model. Since then, this model has experienced dazzling growth with medium-haul flights (flights of less than 3 h), and some low-cost airlines now rival the sector's historical leaders in size: in 2023, Southwest—with 137 million passengers—and Ryanair—with 181 million passengers—were among the world's 10 largest airlines in terms of number of passengers carried. After taking stock of the growth of this model, we analyze its operating levers, before distinguishing two *low-cost* models: *ultra-low-cost* and middle-cost. We conclude with a discussion of the competitive response of the incumbent airlines to the arrival of low-cost carriers.

P. Chiambaretto, E. Combe, *Introduction to Air Transport*, SpringerBriefs in Business, https://doi.org/10.1007/978-3-031-99936-9_4

4.1.1 The Rise of Low-Cost Air Travel

Launched in 1971, Southwest began by operating flights within the state of Texas, on the Austin–San Antonio–Dallas triangle. On the verge of bankruptcy in 1974, the company was forced to reduce its fleet from four to three Boeing 737s and take a daring gamble: offer the same flight schedule with one less aircraft. To achieve this, the company decided to drastically reorganize its business model, reducing stopover time to 20 min, checking tickets directly on board, and reducing passenger service. Thanks to the deregulation of American skies in 1978, Southwest Airlines enjoyed rapid growth in the domestic market and covered the entire country. By 2023, it was serving more than 100 destinations and operating a fleet of 817 aircrafts, making it the world's leading *low-cost* airline.

In the wake of Southwest's success, other *low-cost* airlines entered the US market in the 1980s and 1990s, but with a high bankruptcy rate. Today, the *low-cost* US market essentially comprises six low-cost airlines operating domestically and on the North American continent (Mexico and Canada): Southwest Airlines, Allegiant Air, JetBlue, Frontier Airlines, Alaska Airlines, and Spirit Airlines.

In Europe, *low-cost* flights began in the late 1980s, with the Irish airline Ryanair (founded in 1985 initially as an airline specializing in the transport of business travelers) and the British airline EasyJet (launched in 1995). After the deregulation of intra-European airspace in 1993, *low-cost* air travel grew rapidly: its market share rose from 1.6% of intra-European traffic in 1998 to more than 30% in 2022 (see Fig. 4.1). It should be noted, however, that the low-cost footprint remains fairly differentiated across Europe: while it is predominant in the United Kingdom, Ireland, Spain, and Italy, its presence in Germany and France remains more limited. In terms of players, while a dozen of *low-cost* airlines operated in Europe in 2023, the two pioneers, Ryanair and EasyJet, alone accounted for 50% of traffic.

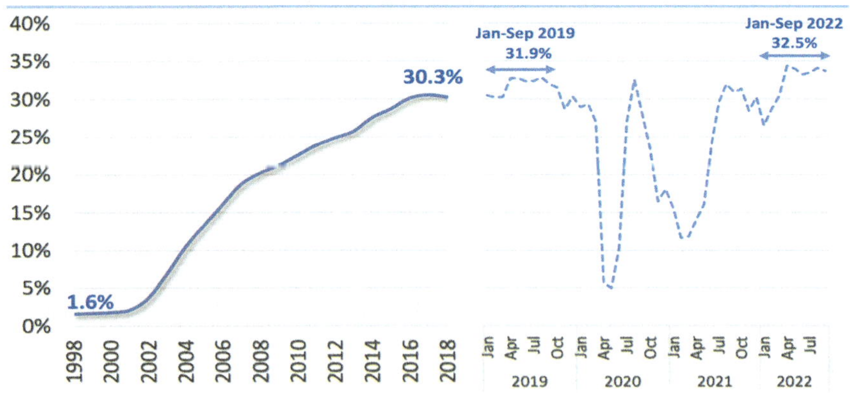

Fig. 4.1 Market share of low-cost carriers in total European flights (%). Source: Pilot Career News (2022), from IATA

Beyond the United States and Europe, *low-cost* carriers have also been developing since the 1990s in countries such as Australia and Japan. Australia, for example, has Virgin Australia and Jetstar, the *low-cost* subsidiary of the national carrier Qantas.

Low-cost air travel is also developing in the emerging countries of Asia and Latin America, while Africa and the Middle East remain relatively unaffected. In Brazil, for example, GOL Airlines rapidly established itself on the domestic market in 2001 and, in 2007, even took over the bankrupt incumbent Varig Airlines. In Asia, *low-cost* airlines are expanding in countries such as Malaysia (with AirAsia X), Indonesia (with Lion Air), India (SpiceJet, Air India Express, and IndiGo), and, more recently, China (a dozen airlines, including Spring Airlines).

4.1.2 A Low-Cost, Minimalist Model

Contrary to popular belief, the low-cost model is primarily driven not by low costs but by a redefinition of consumers' needs in a minimalist sense, such that they only pay for what they consume. This simplification of supply, in turn, leads to a reduction in unit production costs and, therefore, to a reduction in prices, resulting in higher volumes. The coherence of the *low-cost* model lies in the five-step sequence shown in Fig. 4.2, to which we add the roles of outsourcing of fixed costs and paying options.

The low-cost model begins by redefining customer needs (step 1) and the specifications of the product (step 2) in a minimalist way. A traditional airline ticket is made up not only of a main service—traveling from point A to point B quickly and safely—but also of multiple secondary services. An airline ticket can be represented as a flower, with each petal representing a secondary service (Fig. 4.3). The approach of a *low-cost* airline is precisely to peel back the petals of the flower to concentrate on its core promise.

So, unlike traditional carriers, the "pure" *low-cost* model offers customers only "point-to-point" flights, that is, those without any connections, thus avoiding the costs of coordinating flights (e.g., handling delays and baggage). These airlines also avoid using major hubs, concentrating instead on so-called secondary airports, to avoid the constraints of traffic congestion and reduce airport taxes. For example, Ryanair is based in Beauvais, on the outskirts of Paris, but does not operate directly to the capital's two major airports.

In the same spirit, *low-cost* airlines offer a single class, based on the principle that on medium-haul flights, customers expect efficiency rather than comfort. They also densify the number of seats available; that is, in the same aircraft model, they offer more seats, for example, by reducing the "seat pitch" (the distance between two rows of seats). Tickets are booked exclusively through direct sales on their own websites: this "disintermediation" of sales avoids the need to pay commissions to intermediaries such as travel agencies or centralized reservation systems (GDSs). Check-in baggage and catering services are also not included in the ticket price. The

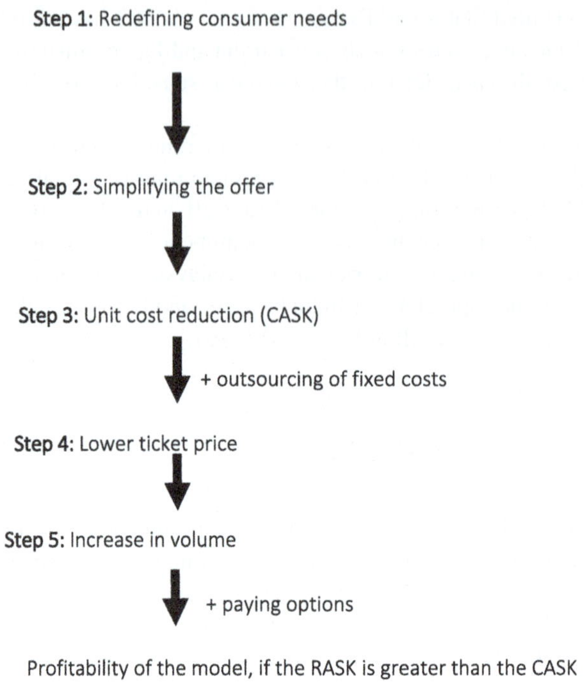

Fig. 4.2 The *low-cost* model. Source: Adapted from Combe (2019)

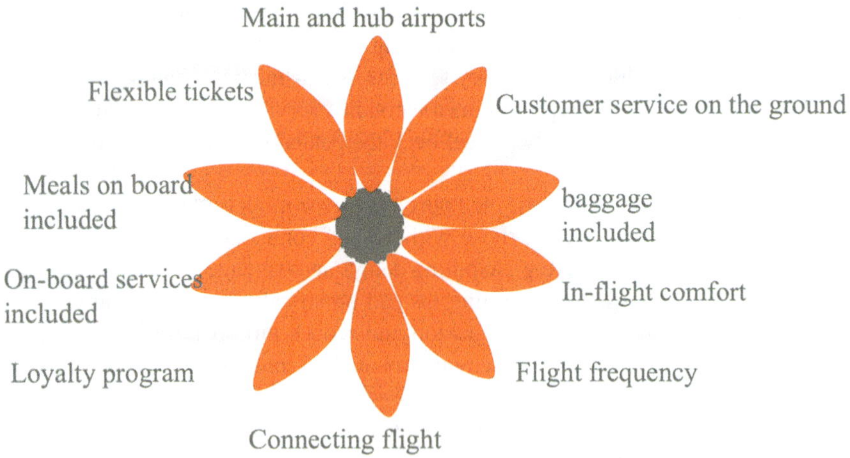

Fig. 4.3 Secondary services included in a "classic" air ticket. Source: Combe (2019)

catering offer is simplified, with basic products (e.g. coffee) to avoid logistical costs between flights (e.g., aircraft restocking of food, cleaning).

Simplifying the product offer helps reduce unit production costs (step 3). In particular, by serving smaller airports, an aircraft operated by a low-cost carrier can make a turnaround (i.e., the time between two flights) in around 30 min, compared with 1 h for a conventional airline, thus optimizing fixed costs. The aircraft is also used intensively, flying up to 12 h a day, compared with 9 h on average for a traditional airline on a medium-haul flight.

This higher aircraft productivity is reinforced if low-cost airlines operate only one type of aircraft (usually Boeing 737s or Airbus A320s), which reduces maintenance, spare parts storage, and crew training costs. The scope of fixed costs is also limited for *low-cost* airlines. With the exception of aircraft and flight crews, *low-cost* carriers outsource most of the typical fixed costs for airlines, to transform them into variable costs. These costs include aircraft maintenance, pilot and cabin crew training and recruitment, and ground services. The same applies to marketing and advertising functions, as well as functions that do not constitute an airline's core business.

The average hourly pay for flight crews is lower than that of incumbent airlines because they fly more hours per year. Remuneration policies also put considerable emphasis on variable pay, indexed to performance indicators: at Ryanair, variable pay can account for up to 50% of total remuneration. Unionization rates are generally low, and some European *low-cost* airlines have even been criticized for their aversion to union rights. A company like Ryanair may sometimes also use subcontractors to provide pilots and cabin crew: this outsourcing strategy transforms a fixed cost into a variable one.

The improved profitability of fixed costs and the reduction in variable costs leads, as we found in Chap. 3, to a sharp drop in CASK, which on average is 2–3 times lower than that for a traditional airline, for an equivalent distance.

Lower unit costs lead *low-cost* airlines to lower ticket prices (step 4). Of course, this average reduction in ticket price does not rule out dynamic pricing (see Chap. 3): ticket prices vary over time, depending on parameters such as the date of booking in relation to the date of the flight. The price of a *low-cost* ticket may therefore be very high, for example, if the customer books at the last minute and in high season: in other words, *low cost* does not always mean low *fare*. A low-cost carrier can even charge high prices when it has a monopoly on a route or when demand is high. The ticket price does not include additional services, such as checked baggage or in-flight catering. When comparing ticket prices between low-cost airlines and traditional airlines, taking into account equivalent services is therefore necessary (see Table 4.1).

Lower ticket prices translate into higher demand (step 5), in particular by encouraging some customers who have not previously flown a particular route to do so. This "induction effect" is particularly marked in the case of *low-cost* airlines operating tourist routes, for which the price elasticity of demand is high. For example, on the London–Barcelona route, EasyJet's entry in 1995, in the face of the Iberia–British Airways duopoly, led to a sharp increase in traffic, which multiplied fivefold

Table 4.1 Comparative analysis of the two models

	Traditional carrier	*Low-cost* carrier
Type of airport	Main airport	Secondary airport (if possible)
Flight organization	Flights with hub connections	Point-to-point
Flight distance	Short-, medium-, and long-haul	Medium-haul
Main target customers	High-contribution passengers (business travelers)	Tourist and affinity customers (second homes, family and friends)
Aircraft fleet	Heterogeneous	Homogeneous and low average age
Onboard catering	Included in ticket price	Minimalist on-board paying option
Offer segmentation	Segmentation into several classes	A single class
Reservation modes	Internet, proprietary agencies, travel agencies, by telephone	Company websites
Aircraft management (short-/medium-haul)	9 h on average per day	Up to 12 h a day
Seating capacity	Standard capacity	Densification of seats
Flight management	Turnaround in less than an hour	Rotation in 30 min
Aircraft load factor	Approximately 85%	More than 90%
Employee compensation	Low proportion of variable compensation	High variable component, based on performance indicators
Unionization rate	High	Low

Source: The authors

in 10 years. In some cases, *low-cost* carriers have actually created their own market after uncovering latent demand: for example, on international routes to Bergerac (mainly from the United Kingdom), traffic rose from 16,000 passengers in 2000 to 315,000 in 2017, a 19-fold increase. While traditional airlines essentially perceive low-cost airlines as competitors (substitution effect), the effect of inducing or generating new demand should not be underestimated.

4.1.3 The Two Faces of Low Cost

The low-cost business model is not homogeneous, enabling distinguishing between "middle-cost" and "ultra-low-cost." This distinction is based primarily on differences in cost and revenue levels, but also on network structure and customer targets (Table 4.2).

The ultra-low-cost model includes airlines such as Ryanair, Wizz Air, and Pegasus in Europe and Spirit Airlines in the United States. These airlines operate with a low-unit-cost base (measured in CASK), of the order of 2.5–3 cents. This cost base is almost three times lower than that of a traditional carrier and twice as low as that of a middle-cost airline.

Table 4.2 The main differences between ultra-low-cost and middle-cost models

	Ultra-low-cost airline	*Middle-cost* airline
Type of airport	Secondary airport	Main airports
First target customers	Tourist customers	Business and VFR customers
CASK	Low (3 cents in 2019)	Higher (5–6 cents in 2019)
Share of variable costs	Above market average	In line with market average
Average ticket price	Low prices	Intermediate prices
Airport subsidies	Frequent	Low
Role of ancillary revenues	High (>30% of sales)	Intermediate (<20%)
Network configuration	Multiple bases at regional airports	Few bases at major airports
Degree of competition with incumbent operators	Low	High
Profitability	Above market	In line with market standards
Flight frequency on a route	Low	High
Flight crew compensation	Below market; high variable portion for cabin crew	In line with market standards
Unionization rate	Low	In line with market standards

Source: The authors

This model is characterized by a low level of fixed costs compared with variable costs, allowing great flexibility in case of shocks. Fuel is the main cost item for Wizz Air (29% in 2019) and Ryanair (35%), far ahead of personnel costs, which account for just 10% of total costs for Wizz Air and 13% for Ryanair.

On the revenue side, ultra-low-cost airlines offer very low prices: at Ryanair, the average ticket was €37 in 2019, plus €17 in paid options, for €54 in total. Ultra-low-cost airlines often boast higher profit margins than other operators, such as Ryanair, whose margin rate fluctuates between 12% and 15% depending on the year.

In terms of network structure, the ultra-low-cost carriers connect myriad regional cities, like Ryanair, which in 2024 had more than 90 bases throughout Europe, or Wizz Air, which had 25 bases, 23 of which were in Eastern Europe. By locating their operations at regional airports, these carriers try to limit taxes, benefit from public subsidies to open new routes, and enjoy a high degree of operational agility.

This type of *low-cost* carrier does not compete head-to-head with traditional airlines, and it sometimes even has a monopoly on a destination, as on the London–Bergerac route operated solely by Ryanair. *Ultra-low-cost* airlines rely primarily on an induction effect: by offering low prices, they create demand in the market, by attracting people who would not otherwise have flown. The target customers are tourists, young people, "affinity" customers, or residents (also known as VFR or "visiting friends and relatives"); flight times and frequency are not a priority for them. Conversely, business customers, who are very sensitive to travel time, flight frequency, and flight schedules, are not attracted to secondary airports, which are often far from major cities. However, business customers may use *ultra-low-cost* flights when they offer rapid access to secondary cities or if they are employed by small companies with limited travel budgets. Ryanair is developing its business model to reduce its dependence on tourists, by setting up operations at major airports such as Rome and Madrid.

The strength of the ultra-low-cost model lies in the consistency between the structure of its offer, in terms of costs and routes offered, and that of demand, in terms of customers and revenues.

A second model is the middle-cost, represented in Europe by airlines such as EasyJet, Transavia, and Vueling and in the United States by JetBlue and Southwest Airlines. These airlines have a unit cost excluding fuel (CASK) of around 5 cents, 60% higher than that of an ultra-low-cost airline. However, this unit cost remains 20–30% lower than that of a traditional airline. A higher unit cost led to an average one-way ticket price with options of around €77 (€61 plus €16 in paid options) in 2019 (25% more than ultra-low-cost carriers).

The higher unit cost of middle-cost airlines is largely due to their base at major airports, where taxes and charges are higher and for which they do not benefit from public subsidies in Europe. They also have fewer bases than ultra-low-cost airlines: in 2024, EasyJet had 30 bases in Europe, compared with more than 90 for Ryanair.

Middle-cost carriers also often find themselves in head-to-head competition with incumbent airlines on routes such as Paris–Nice or Paris–Toulouse, where they compete with Air France. The customer profile of middle-cost carriers is more diversified than that of ultra-low-cost carriers: it includes tourists and VFR customers, as well as business customers who are less price-sensitive but highly destination-dependent. This more "business-like" profile means that middle-cost airlines need to take off from major airports and offer frequent flights at suitable times, so as to be able to make a round trip in a day. It also means focusing on developing loyalty programs and making travel easier by investing massively in digital technology, value-added services (e.g., lounge, speedy boarding), and ticket flexibility.

Like the ultra-low-cost model, the middle-cost model offers a coherent structure between its offer, in terms of costs and routes offered, and demand, in terms of customers and revenues: unit costs are higher, but this is offset by higher unit revenues.

4.1.4 Reaction of Incumbent Airlines to Low-Cost Carriers

The arrival of low-cost carriers has led to a sharp increase in competition on many routes operated by incumbent airlines, which have responded by implementing five main strategies: adaptation, market exit, confrontation, differentiation, and duplication.

The first strategy involves adapting to the new market configuration by lowering prices on routes competing with a *low-cost* airline. This pricing behavior is fairly consistent with the conclusions of microeconomic theory: in a Cournot oligopoly situation, when a new player enters a route, competitors adapt by adjusting their prices downward. Several empirical studies have demonstrated the impact of competition on incumbents' ticket prices: in the United States, Southwest Airlines' entry on an identical route systematically led incumbents to adjust their prices downward by approximately 46%, as illustrated in Table 4.3 (Morrison, 2001). The effect on ticket prices is not limited to routes in direct competition with *low-cost* carriers; it also spreads to the entire air transport market, through what is known as the "Southwest effect." Even when Southwest Airlines is not present on a route between point A and point B, it encourages incumbent airlines to lower their prices, to prevent a future entry. This happens when Southwest is already present on other routes departing from airports A and B (–33%) or when it is present at a nearby airport (–13.1%). This effect is in line with what is predicted by the theory of "contestable markets": the mere possibility of a new player entering the market forces incumbent airlines to take account of this "potential competition" and preventively adjust their prices downward.

The second strategy is to exit the line when the difference in production costs is too great. Suppose, for example, that an incumbent airline has a CASK of 10 cents. Then, an *ultra-low-cost* carrier enters the market with a CASK of 3 cents and charges a monopoly price of 8 cents per kilometer (i.e., below the unit cost of the incumbent). In economics, this is known as "drastic innovation" (Tirole, 1988): the reduction in cost is so great that the new entrant replaces the incumbent, which is forced to exit the market. This type of market configuration occurred in the past, on routes from Marseille to the North-African countries: following the entry of Ryanair, the incumbent Air France stopped its direct flights.

The third strategy is to engage in confrontation with low-cost carriers, with the aim to force them out of the market. In particular, the incumbent may engage in "predatory pricing," in which it lowers prices sharply to put pressure on the new entrant, before raising them in a second phase, when the low-cost airline has existed the market. This strategy is based on sacrificing profits in the short run, with the intent of recouping this loss in the longer run. Take, for example, the case of airlines A and B (see Fig. 4.4). At the competitive equilibrium, the two airlines set price P_C and make an individual profit $\prod^C$. Airline A decides in t' to lower its price to P_W and incurs losses (i.e., a negative profit, equal to $\prod^W$) until t*, the date when its competitor B leaves the market. After t*, airline A finds itself in a situation of monopoly and can then increase its price to P^M and obtain a monopoly profit $\prod^M$.

Table 4.3 The impact of potential and actual competition on airfare

Type of competition	Effect on fares
Actual competition	
Same departure and arrival airport	–46.2%
Same departure airport/substitutable arrival airport	–26.4%
Substitutable departure and arrival airports	–15.4%
Potential competition	
Same departure and arrival airport	–33.0%
Same departure airport/substitutable arrival airport	–13.1%

Source: Morrison (2001)

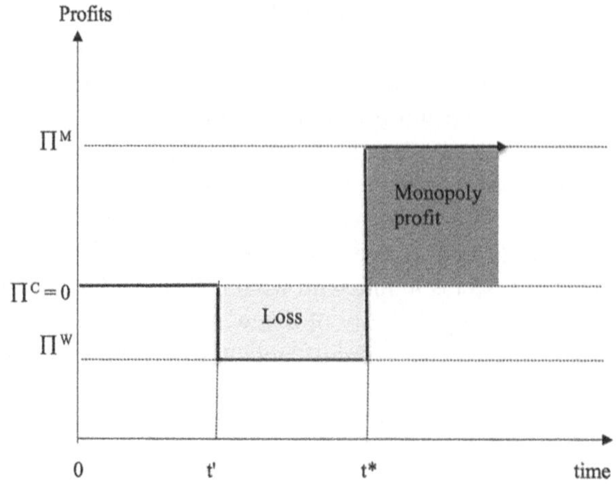

Π^C: competitive profit; Π^W: predatory profit; Π^M: monopoly profit

Fig. 4.4 The predatory pricing strategy. Source: Combe (2021)

This pricing strategy may be completed by a policy of predation through capacity, with the incumbent airline increasing the number of seats available on the route. Both price and capacity predation are difficult to implement in practice, as there is nothing to prevent the *low-cost* carrier from re-entering the market. Moreover, such predation is deemed by antitrust laws as a form of abuse of a dominant position (see Chap. 2).

The fourth strategy relies on product differentiation to avoid head-to-head competition with *low-cost* carriers: the more different customers perceive their services to be, the more the incumbent airline will be able to retain them and justify a higher price. This is a classic microeconomic strategy: product differentiation helps limit price competition. In the case of air transport, product differentiation focuses primarily on business customers, the least price-sensitive segment and the one most in need of a wide variety of services. Incumbent airlines have multiple ways of differentiating themselves from *low-cost* carriers:

- *Presence at a hub*: landing at a *hub* is valued by connecting passengers who want to minimize waiting and travel times between two flights. There is thus a "*hub* premium. »
- *Image*: a "flagship" company can reassure customers.
- *Flight frequency*: this flexibility enables customers to change or postpone their departure time in case of unforeseen circumstances and is a major advantage for business customers.
- *Ground and in-flight services*: conventional airlines offer a wide range of services, some of which are included in the price of the ticket (in particular, in-flight services).

- *Loyalty program*: in particular, business customers, whose tickets are paid for by the company, value the possibility of accumulating loyalty points that they can then use for personal purposes.
- *Control of a large portfolio of takeoff slots at a major airport*: This historical advantage, which cannot be reproduced, makes it possible to offer attractive timetables for morning and end-of-day flights, thus enabling medium-haul flights to make a round trip within the day.
- *A broad portfolio of destinations*: hub systems and commercial alliances with other airlines, especially on long-haul routes, provide customers with many destinations.

The fifth strategy is duplication, by adopting a *low-cost* model, notably on the medium-haul point-to-point market, while retaining a more traditional positioning on long-haul and hub-feeder flights. This strategy tackles the source of the performance differential between low-cost and traditional airlines—namely, CASK. As transforming a traditional airline into a *low-cost* one is particularly difficult—according to the adage "you're born *low-cost*, you don't become low-cost"—a first means is to buy a *low-cost* airline, as the IAG group (British Airways) did when it took control of the *low-cost* airline Vueling in 2013. A second means is to create, ex nihilo, a new dedicated subsidiary within the incumbent carrier: for example, Air France has had its own *low-cost* subsidiary, Transavia France, since 2007. This duplication strategy is difficult to implement for four reasons:

1. To avoid the risk of cannibalization, incumbent airlines have long confined their *low-cost* subsidiaries to destinations they did not serve themselves. For example, Transavia France acted as a "complementary" operator to its parent company: until 2019, none of the scheduled routes operated by Transavia were in direct competition with routes served by Air France/KLM. This situation has since changed, however.
2. Incumbent operators often continue to supply their hubs under their own brand name and thus find themselves having to manage two medium-haul airlines.
3. It's socially difficult for two models to coexist within the same group: employees of the historical subsidiary perceive the *low-cost* subsidiary as a challenge to their status and benefits. To match the DNA and agility of the *low-cost* model, it is necessary to set up a low-cost subsidiary that is sufficiently watertight and autonomous from the parent company.
4. Incumbents, even when they split up, find themselves in an asymmetrical situation with *low-cost* operators: the latter are "pure players," born with the *low-cost* model itself. This means they don't have to learn the ropes of the low-cost model, manage the costs of transition, or coexist with two models.

On the European market, incumbent operators have been ramping up their low-cost subsidiaries since the mid-2010s. However, they have not yet managed to match the size of the *low-cost pure players*, who have had a head start in launching their model: in 2023, if we consider the number of aircraft, the fleets of Vueling (123 aircrafts), Eurowings (100 aircrafts), and Transavia France (90 aircrafts) appear to be modest in size, compared with those of pure players such as Ryanair (563 aircrafts) and EasyJet (336 aircrafts).

4.2 Long-Haul: From Upmarket to Niche Strategies

While on the short- and medium-haul markets almost all players have opted for a strategy of cost domination, the situation appears more contrasted on the long-haul market (flights over 4 h) and, in particular, on long intercontinental flights. On the one hand, many airlines are seeking to implement differentiation strategies, by focusing on upgrading their offer. On the other, some airlines are seeking to adapt low-cost recipes to long-haul routes.

4.2.1 The Choice to Move Upmarket and Differentiate

The strong development of low-cost short- and medium-haul services has transformed air transport into a "commodity." The term "commodity" refers to basic or everyday products (e.g., rice, petrol) whose quality is known and relatively standardized, so that consumers' main criterion of choice is price.

But traditional airlines, unlike low-cost carriers, are also very active on long-haul routes. On these markets, competition takes a completely different form: while prices continue to play a role in air travelers' choices, competition from low-cost airlines is more limited, so airlines can implement strategies that put greater emphasis on product quality.

The stakes are high for traditional airlines, as they make most of their profits on long-haul markets. Figure 4.5 shows the profit per seat in 2023 for the three main European airlines (Air France, British Airways, and Lufthansa), according to their geographic region. On average, while these airlines lose money on short- and medium-haul flights (Europe), they are profitable on long-haul flights (destinations outside Europe).

Given this context, why don't traditional airlines just fly long-haul? These airlines have maintained their short- and medium-haul networks, despite their losses, for two main reasons. First, it is precisely because airlines have a short- and medium-haul network that feeds their long-haul flights that the latter are profitable (see Box 4.1). Indeed, on average, on a long-haul flight (e.g., London–New York), almost 50% of passengers are connecting (i.e., they started their flight before London and/or will end it after New York). Without these short- and medium-haul flights, the long-haul flight would have far fewer passengers, and because of its lower load factor, it would be less profitable. The second reason is more political: many short- and medium-haul routes play a role in opening up regions and are maintained more for their local economic impact than for their profitability.

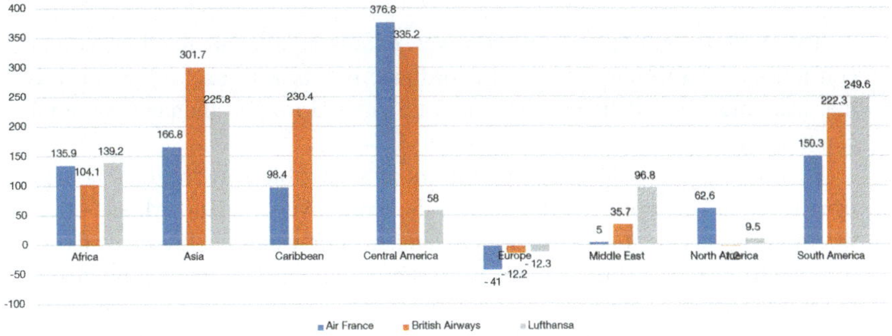

Fig. 4.5 Profit per seat on long-haul routes (2023). Source: The authors, based on RDC Apex 2024

Box 4.1 The hub-and-spoke principle

Traditional airlines are organized on the "hub-and-spoke" principle, which brings together many short- and medium-haul flights at a central point (e.g., Barcelona–Madrid), which then feed into long-haul routes (e.g., Madrid–Buenos Aires).

The advantages of this organization can be illustrated with a numerical example. Suppose an airline wants to serve N cities. If the airline organizes direct flights between each city, it must provide N(N – 1)/2 connections. For example, with 6 cities, the airline has to plan 15 direct connections, which is not necessarily profitable if passenger volume between certain cities is limited.

Another solution is to select the city that generates the most traffic and transform it into a network *hub*: every flight now passes through this central point. This hub system offers several advantages: to serve N cities, only (N – 1) connections are needed: in our example of 6 cities, 5 connections instead of 15 are sufficient. Aircraft load factors increase, as a single flight brings together not only passengers going to the hub but also those connecting from the hub. The hub thus makes it possible to benefit from economies of scale on a flight. For connecting passengers, if the distance traveled increases (because of the *hub*), this inconvenience is offset by higher flight frequency. Indeed, in our example, with 5 connections instead of 15, flight frequency can potentially be multiplied by three.

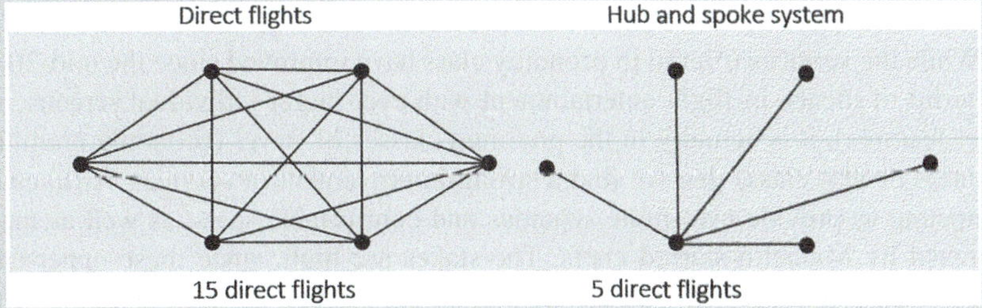

This *hub-and-spoke* system, however, entails significant fixed costs and constraints for airlines: they must coordinate flights with each other, ensure that customers and their baggage are well catered to, and manage potential chain delays and flight cancellations.

By offering more destinations in a more accessible way, airlines benefit from so-called network effects. That is, the more diversified an airline's offer, the more attractive it will be for passengers. For example, frequent flyers wanting to join an airline's frequent-flyer program have an interest in choosing the airline with the most destinations, for two reasons: (1) to earn miles more easily, since an airline offering more destinations is more likely to meet all their needs, and (2) to use the accumulated miles, since they are more likely to find a destination that meets their needs in the airline's varied offers.

In the long-haul market, rather than engaging in a price war, most airlines have opted for a strategy of differentiation. Differentiation entails proposing an offer whose uniqueness will be strongly recognized by customers, who will therefore be willing to pay more to fly with that airline.

Differentiation can be based on multiple factors: the quality of in-flight service, the quality of meals offered, the professionalism of crews, the type of aircraft, seat size, free Wi-Fi access on board, the image of the airline's country of origin, punctuality, and so on. The aim is to appear in consumers' minds as the benchmark airline on these different dimensions. Differentiation involving offering a different service or product, without necessarily making it objectively better (e.g., by emphasizing the airline's nationality), refers to horizontal differentiation. Conversely, differentiation in terms of different levels of quality (e.g., wider or narrower seats) refers to vertical differentiation. In this way, airlines gamble that air passengers will be willing to pay more for their tickets to fly with a particular airline because of its superior services, which in turn leads to customer loyalty. In other words, a strategy of vertical differentiation enables airlines to extricate themselves from price competition.

Initiated by the Gulf airlines (Emirates, Qatar Airways, and Etihad Airways) in the 2000s, this move upmarket (high-end differentiation) by airlines has had the effect of outbidding passengers. Every year, airlines follow the rankings proposed by Skytrax, which rates and classifies airlines by their performance in different classes of travel.

While the services offered in economy class have improved since the mid-2000s (in terms of meals, in-flight entertainment with ever-larger individual screens, and other features), it is actually in the premium classes of travel (economy premium, business or first class) that we find a strong improvement in services. Airlines are competing to provide ever more spacious and comfortable seats, as well as meals designed by Michelin-starred chefs. The stakes are high, since these upper-class passengers, who represent only 20–25% of all passengers, generate 60–70% of the revenue from a long-haul flight. Every effort is therefore made to attract and retain these passengers.

4.2.2 The Long-Haul, Low-Cost Challenge

For a long time, *low-cost* operators targeted the medium-haul market (flights of less than 4 h). However, the early 2000s in Asia and 2010 in Europe saw the arrival of long-haul, *low-cost* flights. In 2004, Qantas launched its Jetstar Airways subsidiary, which operates flights from Australia to Southeast Asia and Japan. In 2011, Singapore Airlines launched its long-haul, *low-cost* subsidiary Scoot. In Europe, development of the long-haul, *low-cost* option is a more recent phenomenon, appearing in 2013, particularly on the transatlantic market, with airlines such as Level, Norwegian, French Bee, and Eurowings. It is worth noting that these *low-cost* airlines are often backed by air transport groups, whether *low-cost* or not, of which they are a dedicated subsidiary.

Yet, while low-cost has made a real breakthrough on short- and medium-haul routes, its impact on long-haul routes appears to be fairly limited for the time being, with a market share generally below 10%. Indeed, the medium-haul, low-cost giants—notably EasyJet and Ryanair in Europe and Southwest Airlines in the United States—have not yet ventured into the long-haul segment, preferring to forge partnerships with airlines specialized in long-haul. Low-cost airlines have been only moderately successful in the long-haul market for several reasons.

First, unlike aircrafts on short- and medium-haul flights, aircrafts are already hitting their maximum potential on the long-haul flights of traditional airlines, so room for improvement by a low-cost airline is limited. Indeed, one of the key factors in the success of low-cost carriers on medium-haul routes is the more intensive use of aircrafts and the higher number of hours flown by crews during the day. However, on long-haul routes (e.g., Rome–New York, Paris–Bangkok), the crews of traditional airlines are already flying within the legal flight time limit, so stringing together two long-haul flights is not possible. Similarly, on these routes, aircrafts are already being used as much as possible and barely have enough time to be cleaned before they're off on the next flight. In other words, the possibilities for cost-cutting operational improvements are lower on long-haul than medium-haul routes.

Second, the low-cost model means a reduction in the passenger experience. However, tolerance for a reduced experience varies depending on the length of the flight. While not having a free drink on a 1-h flight is generally not a problem, not being offered even a free glass of water on a 7- or 8-h flight can be difficult not only in terms of experience but also in terms of passengers' physical safety. As a result, several airlines that have launched long-haul, low-cost flights nevertheless offer free on-board services, which has reduced their ancillary revenues accordingly.

Third, while low-cost carriers offer high-density single cabins on short- and medium-haul routes, this option is more difficult to provide on long-haul routes. As we explained previously, long-haul flights are only really profitable when so-called high-contribution passengers (in business class, for example) pay a high price for their tickets and indirectly subsidize cheaper tickets in economy class. Paradoxically, offering only economy-class seats (as low-cost carriers do on short- and medium-haul routes) would mean raising the price of the ticket. As a result, long-haul, low-cost carriers generally forgo the "one-cabin" principle and offer business-class seats, which raises costs and reduces the number of seats available on the aircraft.

Finally, low-cost carriers tend to offer only direct flights (ideally from secondary airports), so as to avoid dealing with coordination costs and the consequences of a delay on one of the flights. However, long-haul routes generally make a profit from connecting passengers. To guarantee a high-load factor, many of these airlines have opted to set up connecting or self-connecting systems (sometimes even joining forces with other airlines), thereby increasing their costs.

In summary, while several airlines claim to be involved in the long-haul, low-cost option, a more detailed analysis reveals that they are far removed from the "pure" low-cost model and are instead hybrid models. Thus, according to Soyk et al. (2017), on long-haul routes, the potential for cost reduction is of the order of 20–30% compared with a traditional airline, while it exceeds 50% on short- and medium-haul routes. It therefore seems more appropriate to consider these airlines long-haul, middle-cost than long-haul, pure *low-cost*.

4.2.3 The Niche Strategy

Given their high fixed costs, economies of scale, and network effects, most airlines are embarking on a race toward gigantism, offering their passengers evermore destinations and frequencies. Conversely, some airlines have opted for a niche strategy, specializing in a specific customer base to meet their passengers' exact needs, while avoiding head-to-head competition with the most powerful rivals. In air transport, we observe two niche strategies: geographic and customer.

4.2.3.1 Geographic Niche Strategy

Some airlines will essentially offer flights within a given geographic region. These are often regional airlines that play a structuring role in local economic development. This is the case, for example, of Braathens Regional Airlines, a Swedish airline that only offers flights within Scandinavia. This role of connecting territories is all the more important in island regions, where air travel is often the only mode of transport (along with boat travel, which is much slower). In addition, Air Tahiti links the islands of French Polynesia, and Trans Maldivian Airways connects the islands of the Maldives.

Similarly, some international airlines only offer flights to or from a particular region. In France, airlines such as Air Corsica, Air Caraïbes, Corsair, Air Austral, and Air Tahiti Nui play the regional specialization card. In the United States, Alaska Airlines and Hawaiian Airlines follow a similar strategy. Whether American or European, these airlines have two characteristics in common: (1) the desire to concentrate on routes originating or terminating in their own regions, without serving other routes, and (2) the creation of a unique experience for passengers, from the moment they get on the plane, of the airline's home region (in terms of food, uniforms, decoration, passenger gifts, and other features).

Finally, several airlines with no specific regional roots are opening up small, untapped markets. In France, airlines such as Twin Jet, Amélia, and Chalair Aviation operate smaller aircrafts (carrying roughly 10 passengers) and offer air routes between cities for which there is no real alternative by train or car. For example, Chalair offers a route between Lyon and Poitiers, and Twin Jet offers one between Toulouse and Metz-Nancy. On these routes, the airlines have a real competitive advantage, as given the low demand, using a large commercial aircraft is impractical.

These niche airlines often find themselves in a monopoly situation on routes where there is sufficient demand to be profitable, but not too strong to attract a traditional airline. Providing genuine added value to passengers in terms of time, these airlines primarily target the most time-sensitive passengers (i.e., mainly those traveling for business reasons). As these passengers generally have a low price elasticity, setting ticket prices high is a feasible tactic to generate profits.

4.2.3.2 Customer Niche Strategy

Most airlines, whether traditional or low-cost, cater to all passengers, whatever their reason for travel or class of travel. However, some airlines are taking the gamble of focusing solely on certain customer segments, in particular the most profitable ones (i.e., business-class passengers). Adopting this niche strategy, these "100% business" airlines offer flights on which all the seats are business-class seats. While several airlines have attempted this niche strategy in the past (e.g., Eos Airlines, MAXjet Airways), La Compagnie is the only airline in Europe to implement this strategy on all its routes. The airline beOnd, which is structured around a hub in the Maldives, also seems to have a similar business model.

The appeal of this strategy is that, for a traditional airline, business-class passengers, though representing less than 25% of passengers on a long-haul flight, generate 50–70% of the flight's revenue. Business-class passengers therefore subsidize economy-class passengers, who would normally have to pay more for their tickets. The longer the flight, the more pronounced this internal equalization system is: economy-class fares increase less rapidly with distance than business-class fares. If, however, an aircraft has only one business class (single-class configuration), it can significantly reduce the ticket price for passengers, as it does not need to subsidize passengers in economy class. The longer the flight, the more relevant this strategy becomes, as illustrated in Fig. 4.6.

Given its impact on business-class prices, why are so few airlines implementing this niche strategy? First, this strategy is only relevant if a sufficient number of air passengers are traveling in business class. However, only on very few routes are there enough passengers to fill an entire aircraft configured as "100% business class." These carriers often concentrate on a few high-volume transatlantic routes (e.g., Paris–New York), where the majority of business-class passengers are located.

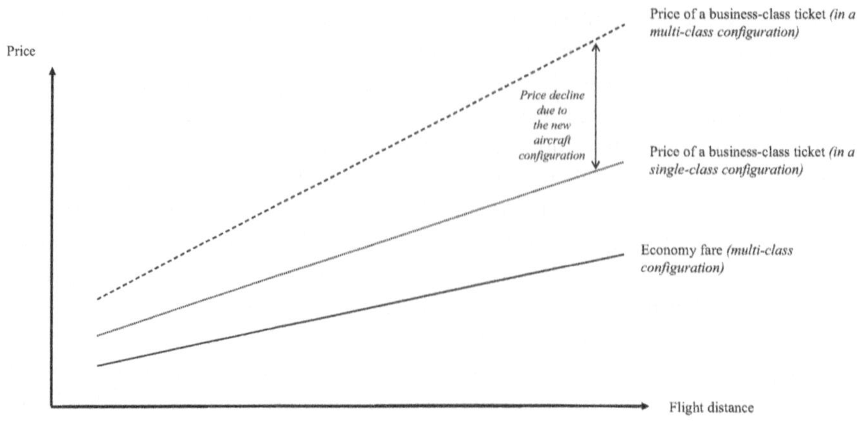

Fig. 4.6 The relationship between economy- and business-class ticket prices and flight distance. Source: The authors

Second, as these airlines concentrate on just a few routes, they have small fleets, so they can only offer one or two flights a day on the route. Business passengers are highly time-sensitive and are often willing to pay more for a flight without waiting several hours. In other words, the lower prices offered by these airlines do not always compensate for the inconvenience caused by lower frequencies.

Finally, these airlines concentrate on a few routes and therefore do not have a wide network of destinations to attract passengers who travel regularly and want to take advantage of the frequent-flyer program to travel elsewhere during their vacations. This makes it more difficult to attract and retain frequent flyers.

References

Combe, E. (2019). *Le low cost*. La Découverte, collection Repères (2nd ed.).

Combe, E. (2021). *Competition policy: An empirical and economic approach*. Wolters Kluwer.

Morrison, S. (2001). Actual, adjacent and potential competition: Estimating the full impact of Southwest Airlines. *Journal of Transport Economics and Policy, 35*, 239–256.

Pilot Career News. (2022). *Eurocontrol: rise of the low cost carriers*.

Porter, M. (1985). *Competitive advantage*. Dunod.

Soyk, C., Ringbeck, P., & Spinler, S. (2017). Long-haul low cost airlines: Characteristics of the business model and sustainability of its cost advantages. *Transportation Research Part A Policy and Practice, 106*, 215–234.

Tirole, J. (1988). *The theory of industrial organization*. MIT Press.

Chapter 5
Future Challenges for Air Transport

Air transport is currently facing three major challenges that are reshaping its ecosystem and casting doubt on its long-term development. The first is climate change, which raises the question of air transport's ability to reduce pollutant emissions. The second challenge relates to changes in air passenger behavior, which could call into question the strategies implemented by airlines over the last few decades. The third challenge is of a geopolitical nature and highlights the growing importance of the air transport sector in terms of the attractiveness and sovereignty of states, with the emergence of new players.

5.1 Air Transport and the Climate Challenge

5.1.1 Air Transport's Share of Emissions

When an aircraft flies, it consumes kerosene and emits greenhouse gases that contribute to global warming. With more than 5 billion passengers expected to fly in 2025 and an annual growth rate of around 4%, the question of the environmental impact of air transport is clearly an important one.

Among the greenhouse gases emitted by aviation are carbon emissions (CO_2), which have been shown to play an important role in global warming. The challenge is to assess the specific contribution of air transport to CO_2 emissions. A consensus among researchers is that air transport accounts for between 2% and 3% of CO_2 emissions worldwide (Lee et al., 2021). This share may vary from country to country and appears to be higher in developed countries (where air travel is more widespread) than in developing countries. However, even in developed countries, air transport's share of CO_2 emissions rarely exceeds 5–6%. For instance, in France, air transport accounts for 6.4% of carbon emissions and 4.9% of greenhouse gases (DGAC, 2019).

P. Chiambaretto, E. Combe, *Introduction to Air Transport*, SpringerBriefs in Business, https://doi.org/10.1007/978-3-031-99936-9_5

Indeed, in addition to CO_2 emissions, it is necessary to take into account the impact of other greenhouse gases, the so-called non-CO_2 effects, in the case of air transport. These include condensation trails (observed in the wake of aircraft), nitrogen oxides, and so on. The main difficulty with non-CO_2 effects is measuring them accurately. Some effects can be warming in the short run but cooling in the long run; unlike CO_2 effects, which are relatively well measured, confidence intervals (i.e., measurement uncertainty) for non-CO_2 effects are much wider. Nevertheless, despite this uncertainty, Lee et al. (2021) conclude that the total contribution (CO_2 and non-CO_2) of air transport to global warming is of the order of 3.5%.

If air transport accounts for "only" 2.1% of CO_2 emissions and 3.5% of greenhouse gas emissions, why is it often singled out when it comes to global warming? There are several possible explanations.

First, there is a relative lack of awareness of air transport's contribution to CO_2 emissions and a strong tendency to overestimate it. Chiambaretto et al. (2021) show that 90% of French people overestimate the environmental impact of air transport and that 50% believe that this sector accounts for more than 10% of global CO_2 emissions.

Second, the focus on air transport is pronounced because it embodies a form of globalization that primarily benefits a small segment of the population. Although all socio-professional categories fly, air transport tends to be perceived as the mode of transport for the "rich," even though passengers generally have the same socio-professional profile as high-speed train passengers (Dobruszkes et al., 2022). Attacking air transport is tantamount to pointing the finger at the over-consumption of wealthy people and their greater contribution to greenhouse gas emissions.

Finally, this focus on air transport is due to its strong growth. Although fuel consumption and CO_2 emissions per passenger are falling steadily (–2.6% per year), the strong growth in air traffic (+4.8% per year) is contributing to an increase in total fuel consumption and air transport emissions (+2.1% per year). While some airlines have succeeded in reducing their CO_2 emissions in absolute terms while continuing to increase their passenger numbers, this is not yet the case for the entire air transport sector (see Fig. 5.1).

Therefore, fiscal, regulatory, technological, and societal solutions are required to limit air transport emissions in absolute terms.

5.1.2 What Role Can Tax and Regulatory Solutions Play?

To limit greenhouse gas emissions, public policy needs to make airlines pay for their emissions, so that they integrate this constraint into their business model. This solution is based on the "polluter-pays" principle, widely favored by economists: the emitter (in this case, the airline) responsible for the pollution pays a tax or buys a right to pollute, the amount of which is equal to the social cost it generates for the community. This tax, or right to pollute, will increase its production cost, which will encourage it to be more virtuous in terms of emissions (by changing technology, for

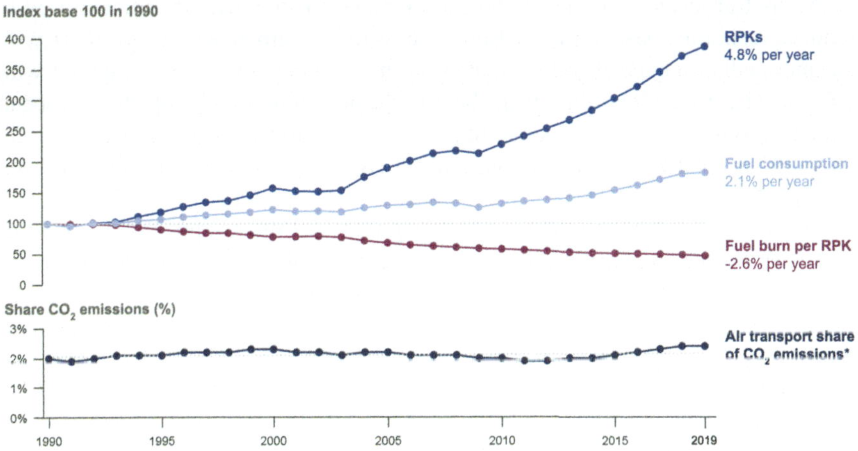

Fig. 5.1 Evolution of air traffic, total fuel consumption, fuel efficiency, and air transport share of CO_2 emissions from 1990 to 2019. Source: Airbus (2024)

example) or to pass on this additional cost to consumers, who will reduce their consumption and, at the same time, the level of CO_2 emissions.

In the case of air transport, the polluter-pays principle has led to the introduction of environmental taxes on airline tickets at the national level. In Sweden, for example, since 2018, all passengers departing from a Swedish airport, on stopovers and, under certain conditions, in transit, must pay a tax, the amount of which varies with distance. Similarly, in France, an environmental tax on air transport, known as an "eco-contribution," has been in force since 2020. It applies to all flights departing from France, with the exception of connecting flights, domestic flights to and from Corsica, overseas territories, and regional development routes. All airlines departing from France, whatever their nationality, are included. As in Sweden, the tax is progressive, but its distinguishing feature is that the amount is differentiated according to whether the passenger travels in economy or business class. The risk of a tax imposed at the national level is that it may be circumvented by some passengers, who may choose to fly to neighboring countries. Opponents of the tax in Sweden, for example, contend that it has encouraged passengers to choose flights and airlines that stop over in Denmark rather than Sweden.

An instrument equivalent to the environmental tax is the "right to pollute," in which companies are authorized by the public authorities to emit a maximum quantity of greenhouse gases each year; here, a certain number of "quotas" or "emission credits," measured in tons of CO_2, are allocated to them, up to the authorized ceiling. If companies exceed their ceiling, they must purchase additional allowances from other companies that have significantly reduced their emissions. A market is set up for trading allowances between companies, with the price per allowance varying by supply and demand. The price rises when there is strong demand for these rights or when the public authorities decide to reduce the cap granted to each company.

At the European Union level, the carbon market is the main instrument used to reduce greenhouse gas emissions. Europe aims to be "carbon neutral" by 2050, with an intermediate target of a 55% reduction in emissions by 2035, compared with 1990 levels. To achieve this goal, the European Union has set up the European Union Emissions Trading Scheme. In practice, the European carbon market covers only 40% of the EU's greenhouse gas emissions, as certain sectors have so far been exempted.

In the case of air transport, pollution rights in Europe apply only to intra-European flights, and airlines have long benefited from free quotas. The situation changed dramatically in 2022: Europe decided to phase out the free allowances granted to airlines by 2026. This change will have a marked impact on the price of intra-European flights, given the high cost of quotas. For example, the average price of an allowance (i.e., a ton of CO_2) rose from €5 in 2014 to €80 by the end of 2022. It is likely that airlines will pass on the cost of pollution rights to customers, in the price of plane tickets, which will limit traffic growth.

The main problem with the European carbon market is that it applies only within Europe, while other regions in the world, such as China, do not impose the same constraints on their domestic markets. This can distort competition if, for example, Europe decides to subject European airlines to a carbon tax on their intercontinental flights. To limit this distortion, the European Union introduced a border carbon adjustment mechanism from 2023 onward, which taxes non-European companies selling in Europe that do not comply with the same environmental standards as those applied in Europe.

A first step toward a global carbon market for all airlines was taken in 2018 with the adoption by ICAO of the CORSIA program (Carbon Offsetting and Reduction Scheme for International Aviation). This program provides for the purchase of emission credits by airlines (in addition to measures to stimulate clean fuels) if they exceed a certain level of permitted emissions. The ultimate goal of the CORSIA program is to achieve carbon neutrality in air transport by 2050 (Scheelhaase et al., 2018). An emissions measurement and verification system is due to be set up by all ICAO member states to ensure that their airlines are on a decarbonization trajectory, failing which they will have to purchase emission credits. Deployment of the CORSIA program is still in its early stages. An initial pilot phase, between 2021 and 2023, brought together 81 countries on a voluntary basis to report their airlines' emissions and impose offsets in the event of overruns. However, it will not be until 2027 that all international flights will be subject to the carbon offset mechanism.

In addition to these incentive instruments, which are based on price signals, another public policy entails banning certain flights in the name of the climate imperative. France, for example, decided to discontinue domestic air services if there was a rail alternative of less than 2 h and 30 min by 2020. The French decision was based on European regulation 1008/2008, which authorizes a member state, under certain conditions, to limit or refuse traffic rights in order to remedy "serious environmental problems." In addition, the regulation stipulates that the restriction must be limited in time and must not go beyond what is necessary. This ban, contested by some airlines, was confirmed by the European Commission in December

2022, on the grounds that it was consistent with the European Union's climate objectives and did not raise competition concerns. This measure has inspired the Spanish government to consider doing the same on some domestic Spanish routes.

5.1.3 *What Role Can Technological Solutions Play?*

Beyond regulatory and fiscal constraints, technological innovation is a lever for reducing the environmental footprint. While as of yet no miracle solution for reducing greenhouse gas emissions has been put forth, the air transport sector is working on a combination of innovations throughout the value chain.

Upstream the value chain, aircraft and engine manufacturers play a key role in developing new technologies that consume less energy and emit fewer greenhouse gases. The IEA (International Energy Agency) highlights a drastic reduction in the energy intensity (and, thus, fuel consumption) of new-generation aircraft during the past 60 years (see Fig. 5.2). This reduction is the result of a combination of factors, including improved aircraft aerodynamics, more fuel-efficient engines, and lighter aircraft.

A first avenue for innovation is improving engine efficiency in terms of fuel consumption. Today, on long-haul flights, aircrafts such as the Boeing B-787 and the Airbus A330neo have very low fuel consumption, of the order of 2.7 liters per passenger per 100 km flown. On short- and medium-haul flights, new-generation aircrafts such as the A320neo and Boeing 737max also consume around 2.2 or 2.3 liters per passenger per 100 km.

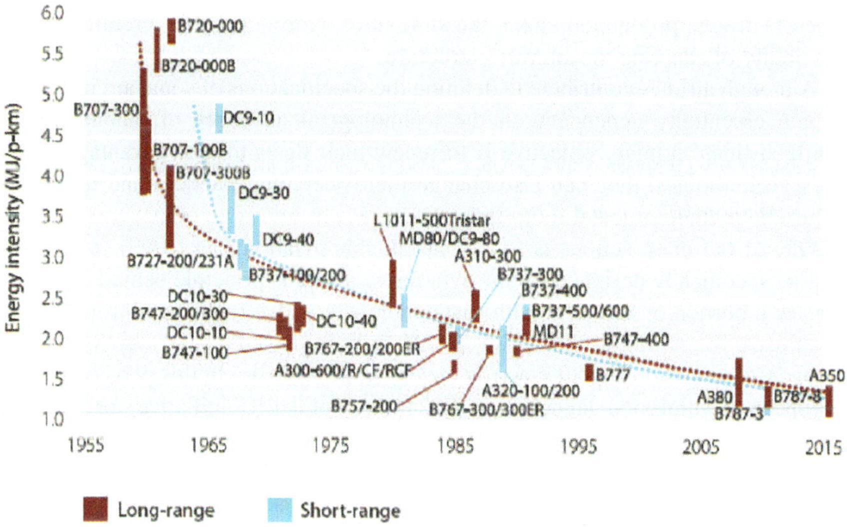

Fig. 5.2 Energy intensity of aircrafts (1955–2015). Source: IEA (2009)

A second avenue for innovation is the increasing use of composite materials in aircraft construction—for example, by integrating carbon or glass fiber. These materials are generally lighter and more resistant to corrosion than the metals traditionally used on aircraft. Until the 1980s, manufacturers used composite materials in secondary parts of the aircraft structure. In 1988, Airbus produced the first commercial aircraft with an all-composite tail: the A320. More recently, manufacturers have extended the use of composites to the fuselage and wings. The Boeing 787, which entered service in 2011, was the first commercial jumbo jet to be built predominantly with composite materials. Alongside the use of these composite materials is the question of how to recycle the materials used when the aircraft reaches its end of life.

A third avenue for innovation is using forms of energy other than kerosene to power aircraft. Two main avenues are currently being explored: electric aircraft and hydrogen-powered aircraft. While there are currently a few electric aircrafts for light aviation (2–4 seats), the technology for producing 100% electric commercial aircraft is not yet mature. Indeed, current technologies could make it possible to develop hybrid aircrafts (with mixed propulsion from both fossil fuels and electric power), but the main obstacle to building totally electric aircrafts lies in the energy efficiency and weight of current batteries. Moreover, electric aircrafts only make sense if the electricity comes from production methods that generate little or no CO_2 (Schäfer et al., 2019). With regard to hydrogen-powered aircrafts, the announcement of the ZEROe program by Airbus in 2020 rekindled interest in hydrogen as an energy source in aviation. Hydrogen can be used to either power jet engines directly or power fuel cells that then generate electricity to power electric motors. The advantage of hydrogen is that it can considerably reduce both CO_2 and non-CO_2 effects, provided that the latter, which does not exist naturally, is produced sustainably. Several criteria must still be met, however, before hydrogen-powered aircrafts can actually be developed (planned for 2035 by Airbus), including the creation of a green hydrogen production chain, the storage of hydrogen in the aircraft, and the possibility of adapting the aircraft's structure.

Although airlines contribute to defining the specifications of some aircrafts, they remain essentially dependent on the technological advances of manufacturers. While airlines' primary objective is to renew their fleets to take advantage of the latest technologies, they can also change their operating practices and models to reduce their environmental footprint.

One of the main actions is to use sustainable aviation fuel (SAF), which is a biofuel specifically designed for the aviation sector. The principle behind SAF is to replace a portion of kerosene with sustainable alternative fuels made from various biomasses. According to the ICAO (2022), a flight powered solely by SAF could reduce CO_2 emissions by 80% across the entire value chain. In this perspective, the European Commission launched in 2021 the ReFuelEU initiative for aviation, which aims to increase both demand for and supply of SAF (see Box 5.1).

However, several challenges need to be overcome. First, SAF requires specific technical and chemical properties that enable it to be used in extreme conditions of temperature or pressure not encountered by other modes of transport. Second, the use of this biofuel is only worthwhile if its production generates as less CO_2 than kerosene production and if it does not compete with human food production on land. With this in mind, the airline industry is complying with regulatory sustainability standards and encouraging the production of biofuel from domestic or agricultural waste. Nevertheless, the need for biomass to produce sufficient levels of SAF at the European or global levels clearly exceeds the available biomass. (The same challenge appears with synthetic SAF, which does not require biomass but a significant amount of electricity to be produced.) Similarly, the establishment of an economically viable and sustainable industry is a prerequisite for accelerating the use of sustainable biofuel in aviation and thus reducing net CO_2 emissions from air transport. Last, SAF is considerably more expensive to produce than traditional kerosene. In the absence of tax incentives, its use remains costly and therefore limited for many airlines.

Box 5.1 The ReFuelEU aviation initiative

The ReFuelEU aviation regulation, adopted in 2021, mandates that all fuel in EU airports contains a minimum share of SAF by 2025 and, by 2030, a minimum share of synthetic fuel, with both shares increasing progressively until 2050. Airlines will have to incorporate 2% SAF in 2025, 6% in 2030, and 70% in 2050. By 2030, 1.2% of fuel must also be synthetic, rising to 30% in 2050.

According to EASA (2024), 3.2 million tons of SAF are expected to be produced in the EU by 2030 (in the realistic case), with a pipeline of 5.5 Mt of SAF capacity (in the optimistic case). This production should be sufficient to meet the target set for 2030 (2.8 Mt).

The main problem in Europe is the cost of producing SAF, which is very high. According to EASA, the cost of a conventional aircraft fuel in 2023 was 816 EUR/ton on average, compared with 2768 EUR/ton for a SAF and an estimate set between 6600 and 8700 EUR/ton for synthetic fuel (see the figure below). Increased incorporation of SAF and synthetic fuel will therefore logically translate into higher costs for airlines, which will pass them on in the ticket price (see Sect. 5.1.4).

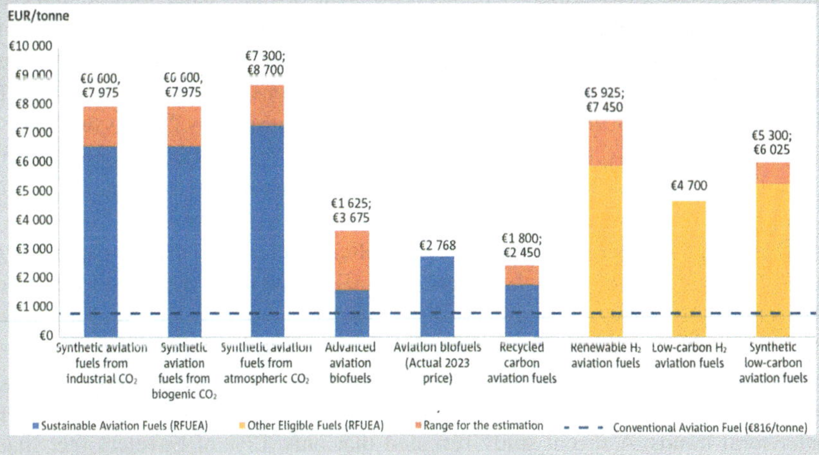

Source: EASA (2024)

The second lever that airlines can mobilize, in addition to technological innovation, is to lighten their aircrafts. According to data provided by Air France as part of its "Horizon 2030" environmental transition plan, lightening each aircraft in the Air France fleet by 1 kilo would save 69 tons of CO_2 per year. With this in mind, several airlines have embarked on this "kilo hunt" to reduce the weight of their aircrafts. Their efforts have focused on requests to manufacturers and service providers to lighten seats, aircraft furnishings, and so on.

A third line of action involves the development of *eco-taxiing*. Indeed, all flights begin and end with more or less long periods of taxiing to connect terminals (or parking areas) to runways. For instance, in France, the average taxiing time in 2018 was 18 min. This taxiing is generally powered by aircraft engines. To reduce their CO_2 emissions during this taxiing phase, some airlines have introduced eco-taxiing procedures. These procedures involve taxiing with only one engine running (single-engine taxiing), which can reduce the associated emissions by almost 50%. Finally, for the longer term, some aircraft manufacturers are considering the introduction of an electric taxiing system, which would make it possible to avoid using aircraft engine power during taxiing.

The last lever that airlines can mobilize is eco-piloting. The premise of eco-piloting lies in the implementation of procedures that are more energy-efficient—for example, by adapting flight speed or altitude or optimizing trajectories. The use software to optimize eco-piloting, however, can only be done in collaboration with air navigation services, which can authorize more direct trajectories and thus contribute to reducing flight times and greenhouse gas emissions.

5.1.4 What Role Can Societal Changes Play?

In parallel with economic and technological measures, an increasing number of stakeholders are advocating for the development of more behavioral and societal initiatives, arguing that economic and technological tools alone are insufficient for the aviation sector to significantly reduce its greenhouse gas emissions. Championed by both researchers and non-government organizations, these critics contend that the only viable path for aviation to achieve carbon neutrality by 2050 is to reduce air travel. In other words, these actors call for "sobriety" or a deliberate contraction in air traffic as a means to substantially lower emissions within the sector (Gössling et al., 2019).

This notion of degrowth implicitly or explicitly references the concept of *flygskam* (or "flight shame"), which reflects a disinclination to fly out of concerns about environmental impacts, compounded by societal pressure to limit air travel. Popularized by environmental activist Greta Thunberg just before the COVID-19 pandemic, *flygskam* has become a significant topic of media attention in recent years. However, this extensive media coverage appears to misrepresent actual behavioral trends. A recent study revealed that only 12% of travelers feel shame when flying (Chiambaretto et al., 2023), and this sentiment of flight shame does not seem to have significantly curbed passenger demand.

Indeed, despite widespread environmental awareness, *flygskam* has had a limited impact on changing travel behaviors, as shown by Schmidt et al. (2024). The persistence of high levels of air travel consumption is explained by the knowledge–action gap (Kollmuss & Agyeman, 2002), which indicates that increased awareness does not necessarily lead to significant behavioral shifts. Only a minor fraction of consumers believe their personal travel choices impact climate change, suggesting a preference for governmental intervention (Mkono, 2020). In addition, inadequate alternatives to flying, such as trains or buses, which are often lacking in comfort, convenience, or cost-efficiency, deter consumers from opting out of air travel (Dällenbach, 2020). Consequently, even the environmentally conscious younger generation continues to travel by air frequently, influenced by the pervasive allure of travel and its promotion on social media (Gössling & Dolnicar, 2022).

Also noteworthy is that, for now, air travelers appear largely unwilling to alter their behavior or bear the additional costs associated with greening aviation. As radically new technologies remain out of reach for the moment, the air transport industry has adopted interim solutions, such as carbon offsetting. This mechanism allows passengers to fund environmental projects like reforestation or renewable energy production to compensate for the carbon emissions from their flights. However, these initiatives are sometimes criticized for their lack of transparency and variable effectiveness. In addition, they rely on voluntary contributions from passengers, who decide the amount they wish to offset in addition to their ticket price. This amount can vary significantly, from less than €1 to €55 per ton of CO_2, influenced by factors such as flight distance, passenger nationality, and the nature of the funded project. Surveys reveal that, on average, less than 5% of passengers opt to offset their emissions (for a review on the topic, see Chiambaretto et al., 2024).

Beyond these measures, the willingness of air travelers to pay more for flights using less polluting technologies, such as SAF, remains an open question. An international study investigating choices made by more than 1100 respondents in 17 countries across the globe found that passengers are willing to pay an extra 10 cents per euro to reduce their CO_2 emissions by 1 kg (Chiambaretto et al., 2024). This willingness varies depending on individual environmental sensitivity and consumption habits. Factors such as *flygskam* and confidence in the aviation industry's ability to address environmental challenges significantly influence passengers' likelihood to pay more for cleaner flights, with some passengers willing to pay up to 27 cents to reduce their emissions by 1 kg.

Given that voluntary approaches do not always yield the desired outcomes, a growing number of airlines, such as Lufthansa, have implemented "environmental surcharges" to pass on the additional costs of these environmental measures directly to customers. In Lufthansa's case, the surcharge will apply to all flights scheduled from 2025 onward, departing from the 27 countries of the European Union.

5.2 Air Transport and New Passenger Behaviors

5.2.1 Business Customers: The Rise of Videoconferencing

By drastically limiting air travel opportunities, the COVID-19 crisis forced business travelers to change their habits, replacing flights with videoconferencing. Initially forced, this replacement has gradually become more permanent, even after air traffic recovered, raising the question of a lasting change in the behavior of business travelers.

While videoconferencing does not replace travel for personal or tourist reasons, it can replace some business trips previously made by air. Although they represent only 20% of air passengers, business travelers are an important target for airlines: they generate between 50% and 70% of some airlines' revenues, since they travel frequently and are not very sensitive to price variations.

Since the 2000s, and even more so since the pandemic, some companies have been encouraging their employees to replace air or rail travel with videoconferencing for several reasons. These include reduced travel costs for the company, a desire to reduce the company's environmental footprint as part of its CSR policy, improved productivity by limiting time wasted on travel, and a better work–life balance.

All these factors have led some observers to predict the end of business travel by air. The reality, however, is more nuanced.

First, forecasts of the decline in business customer traffic show different results for different types of flight: intercontinental flights are more affected than medium-haul flights (Roland Berger, 2022).

Second, not all types of travel can be replaced by videoconferencing, especially those requiring high levels of human interaction, such as maintenance, sales prospecting, trade show participation, and creative meetings (Müller & Wittmer, 2023). Conversely, project follow-up meetings or certain internal trips (between two subsidiaries of the same company) can be replaced by videoconferencing, without reducing the efficiency and quality of the meeting. More generally, a consensus seems to be that videoconferencing is effective for continuing existing projects or between people who already know each other but that it cannot replace travel (by plane or train) to launch new projects or generate trust between members of new teams.

Finally, while the growing use of videoconferencing can improve the work–life balance, it can also generate a form of technostress among employees, who feel they are never disconnected and lose certain advantages associated with a nomadic lifestyle.

Therefore, videoconferencing and air travel will likely serve as complementary modes of communication in the future and may even reinforce each other. For example, Denstadli et al. (2013) show that executives who make the most videoconferences are also those who make the most business trips. In other words, business trips generate videoconferences, which in turn create new opportunities for future travel. The same phenomenon applies to virtual teams, which can only function properly if they meet physically at different stages of a project.

5.2.2 *Leisure Clientele: The Rise of Self-Connecting*

Although tourist traffic remains buoyant worldwide, as evidenced by the strong rebound in leisure travel in the recent post-COVID-19 years, tourist behavior is marked by new phenomena. In particular, some customers are extending the duration of their trip, taking indirect flights, and organizing their own transfers (Fichert & Klophaus, 2016) to reduce the total price of their ticket. This phenomenon, known as "self-connecting," calls into question the system of connections, set up by the long-established airlines through their hubs.

In the traditional model, airlines offer passengers indirect flights via their hub and offer them various services. For example, passengers who want to fly from Manchester to New York can buy a ticket from British Airways, which will offer them a flight from Manchester to London and then a flight from London to New York. This connection model is based on four factors:

1. A single-ticket booking process, from Manchester to New York;
2. Customer care in the event of disruption to one of the flights (e.g., cancellation, delay);
3. Minimized waiting time between two flights; and
4. Easier transit, with automatic baggage transfer between the two flights.

This model is very costly and complex for an airline to manage, since it must coordinate logistics and flights between destinations. All these costs are *ultimately* reflected in the ticket price. The hub model, with its organized connections, is perfectly suited to *business* customers, who want to minimize waiting times between flights, even if it means paying more for the ticket. It is less suited to tourist customers, who tend to be price-sensitive but less concerned with flight times.

Self-connecting behavior has been facilitated by the rise of low-cost airlines, which offer multiple flights to the same airport. They offer customers the option of taking a second flight when booking their ticket, without making any commitment as to the continuity of the service. It's up to customers to organize the best possible transfer between flights. This *self-connecting* strategy enables low-cost airlines to attract additional customers and increase their load factor, without sacrificing flight plan optimization or speed. Self-connecting allows them to benefit from the advantages of an airport's critical size, without the constraints, costs, and responsibilities inherent in the connecting system.

In Europe, airlines such as EasyJet, Vueling, and Ryanair have now reached the critical mass to offer passengers connections to myriad destinations. *Self-connecting* can be between flights of the same airline (e.g., Vueling/Vueling at Barcelona airport), with another airline in the group (Vueling/Level at Barcelona airport), or with another *low-cost* airline. We also observe the practice of self-connecting between a medium- and a long-haul airline. For example, the "Worldwide by EasyJet" offer provides customers at several airports with connections to long-haul flights operated by partners such as Corsair, Virgin Atlantic, and WestJet to key North American destinations.

Self-connecting poses a real threat to incumbent airlines, reducing the attractiveness of their hubs. Indeed, the proliferation of *self-connecting* flights is increasing competition between hubs to attract transit passenger traffic: competition is no longer limited to the major hubs of Frankfurt, Paris Charles de Gaulle, and Heathrow; it also pertains to more "secondary" airports (in terms of traffic) such as Barcelona and Milan. Admittedly, *self-connecting* is not primarily aimed at business customers, but it is certain to weaken economy-class load factors, particularly on long-haul flights.

5.3 Air Transport as an Issue of Sovereignty and Attractiveness

A country's sovereignty in the air transport sector rests first and foremost on its ability to control the upstream phase of aircraft production. In this respect, only the United States and Europe currently enjoy technological sovereignty, making other countries highly dependent on both. For example, since the start of the Russo-Ukrainian War, Russian airlines, whose fleets mainly comprise Airbus and Boeing, have been weakened by the Western boycott of spare parts. Similarly, in the trade war that has pitted it against the United States since 2018, China has also been weakened due to part of its fleet consisting of Boeing or its use of US technologies, particularly in aircraft engines. Under these conditions, it is easy to understand why Russia and China are trying to emancipate themselves from their dependence on European and American technology, by catching up technologically.

A country's air transport sovereignty also depends on the attractiveness of its territory, whether as a host or a transit country, through a major international hub. In this respect, since the early 2000s, the center of air traffic flows has begun to shift eastward, fostering the emergence of new hubs competing with European hubs.

5.3.1 *Manufacturers: Toward Greater Chinese and Russian Sovereignty?*

For a country aspiring to certain independence in air transport, mastering the construction of a range of aircrafts, their engines, and avionics is a must. This requires substantial R&D investment: on average, the cost of developing a new aircraft model is estimated at US$15 billion (Rodrigue, 2020). Not only that, but this investment is quite risky: developing an aircraft model is not only a fixed cost but also a cost that cannot be recouped if the project fails. In addition, development and certification times for a new aircraft are long, often exceeding 10 years.

Given these specific features, it's hardly surprising that the aircraft manufacturing market is a highly oligopolistic one, with a small number of players over the past

50 years. Today, it is dominated by two countries and two manufacturers—the United States with Boeing and Europe with Airbus—which together account for more than 85% of total commercial aircraft orders worldwide. Their market share is higher for wide-body jets than for single-aisle aircraft, where players such as Brazil's Embraer and Canada's Bombardier (whose aeronautics division was acquired by Airbus in 2020) also operate. An oligopoly exists in the aircraft engine construction market, with three main manufacturers dominating the world market: the American Pratt & Whitney, the French Safran associated with the American General Electric, and the British Rolls-Royce.

The dominance of the United States and Europe in aircraft and engine construction creates a highly dependent relationship for third countries, particularly in the event of conflict. For example, since the outbreak of its war with Ukraine in 2022, Russia has been subject to a boycott by Western aviation suppliers of spare parts (needed for aircraft maintenance and repair), engines, and new aircraft. This boycott is a major constraint on Russia's ability to keep its fleet of commercial aircrafts in service, without compromising flight safety.

However, this American and European dominance does not mean that Boeing and Airbus are not also dependent to some extent on their trading partners. For example, the manufacture of an aircraft requires the use of titanium, a metal imported in large part from Russia: 50% of the titanium used by Airbus or Safran comes from the Russian giant VSMPO. Although the European sanctions against Russia, imposed in 2022, do not apply to this metal, the European aerospace industry will have to reduce its exposure to Russian titanium by finding new sources of supply.

Given their heavy dependence on European and American aircraft manufacturers, China and Russia have been trying for many years to emancipate themselves by catching up technologically (Spreen, 2019). Their goal is to have their own aircraft, engine, and avionics manufacturers.

Since the 2000s, China has invested between US$50 and US$70 billion in public funds to develop its first medium-haul commercial aircraft, the C919, developed by state-owned manufacturer Commercial Aircraft Corporation of China (COMAC). Positioned as a competitor to the Airbus A 320 and Boeing 737, this aircraft was certified to fly in Chinese skies in 2022. Its entry into service with Air China in 2024 creates a new competitive landscape for Airbus and Boeing on the Chinese domestic market, the world's largest in terms of size. Over the next 20 years, China's needs are estimated to be more than 9300 aircrafts, or 20% of the world's requirements for new aircraft. China's leading airlines have announced their intention to purchase domestic aircraft from COMAC.

While this is an important technological event, the C919 threat to Airbus and Boeing is rather low, at least for now, and must be put into perspective. First, the C919 is not yet certified outside China. Second, for the moment, the engines powering it are European and American, though the Chinese are developing their own with the state-owned Aero Engine Corporation of China. Third, the C919 remains an assembly of components from multiple countries: of the 82 main parts suppliers for the aircraft, only 14 are Chinese, and of those, half are from joint ventures with foreign companies.

After launching its first medium-haul aircraft, China announced in 2024 its intent to develop its own long-haul aircraft, the C929, which will compete directly with Airbus's and Boeing's largest aircrafts. The development of the C929 was originally planned as a joint venture between Russia and China. However, after the start of the Ukraine conflict in 2022 and the subsequent Western sanctions, the partnership between the two countries was terminated. The loss of the Russian partnership could affect the procurement of certain technologies and components that were originally planned to be supplied by Russian companies. COMAC now must develop all technology and production capabilities in China itself. With a projected seating capacity of around 280 passengers, the C929 will be smaller than rival models (Airbus A350 and Boeing 777) but could be just the right size for the Chinese market and other Asian markets, which are often less densely populated than European and North American routes.

The Russian aircraft manufacturer Sukhoi's military know-how has led to the development of a regional aircraft, the Superjet 100, which entered service in 2011 on the Russian market and in a few neighboring countries, such as Armenia. As in the case of China, the Superjet is powered by a foreign engine manufacturer—namely, Safran. Approximately 70% of the aircraft's equipment, such as avionics and landing gear, is also of European or American origin. The boycott of Russia since 2022 has compromised the continued operation of these aircrafts, as Russia no longer has access to Western spare parts. Russia has embarked on a program to re-engine its entire fleet of Superjet 100s with Russian engines, but according to experts, this will take several years.

A second aircraft project, positioned as a competitor to the Boeing 737 and Airbus A320, was certified by the Russian authorities in 2022: the MC 21, developed by Irkut, a subsidiary of the Rostec space and defense conglomerate. This aircraft was to be equipped with American engines and to incorporate Western components; however, given the boycott of Russia since February 2022, its entry into service is no longer an issue. In a best-case scenario, the MC 21 should enter service in 2025, by which time Russia should have finalized the development of an engine and replaced the Western avionics with those from Indian, Chinese, or Brazilian suppliers.

At the end of this development, China and Russia will still have a long way to go to achieve technological sovereignty. First, it's not enough to develop an aircraft to be independent: the countries also need to be able to produce engines and avionics. Second, the replacement of Airbus and Boeing currently in service in China and Russia will be partial, mainly involving domestic flights. For international flights, the construction of a long-haul aircraft is not yet on the agenda in Russia and China; moreover, it is not certain that the European and American authorities will certify Russian and Chinese aircrafts, thus forcing airlines to retain the use of Airbus and Boeing for international flights.

5.3.2 *Air Transport as a Power Issue*

5.3.2.1 The Emergence of New Hubs

As we noted in Chap. 1, air transport can be a lever of growth and employment for a region or a country, through the establishment of businesses, spending by connecting passengers, and tourism revenues. So, it's easy to understand why some countries choose to invest heavily in their air transport ecosystem, whether in terms of airport infrastructure or airlines.

In this respect, the Netherlands and Singapore have been pioneers: despite their modest size, they have succeeded in building attractive international hubs, backed by a major airline. Schiphol airport, for example, is Europe's third-largest airport, carrying 71 million passengers in 2019, even though the Netherlands has a population of just 17 million. Serving more than 330 destinations in 100 countries, the airport is an important stopover for many airlines linking Asia with North and South America, and it is also the hub for KLM, which attracts customers from all over Europe with medium-haul flights and then offers them long-haul flights.

From the 2000s onward, Middle Eastern countries such as Qatar and the United Arab Emirates have followed a similar path, investing massively in air transport. This proactive policy has been supported by government intervention, using two complementary levers: the creation of major airports and the growth of a national airline, owned or supported by public authorities. Qatar now has a hub in Doha and a Qatar Airways airline, and the United Arab Emirates has developed two hubs: one in Abu Dhabi with Etihad and the other in Dubai with Emirates.

The first objective of these countries was to create giant "hubs" to enable connections between two long-haul flights, by taking advantage of their geographic location, halfway between Asia, Europe, and Africa. This "hub" activity has benefited from a favorable context, with the rise of emerging countries such as China and India in the 2000s. Given the geographic distances involved, long-haul traffic from Asia to Europe, Africa, or the United States favors a stopover. The second objective was to develop local tourist activity and attract foreign investment, particularly in the case of Dubai. According to IATA, in 2019, the aviation and tourism sector accounted for 13% of the GDP of the whole of the United Arab Emirates and more than 800,000 local jobs.

More recently, Turkey has also set its sights on building a giant long-haul hub: the new Istanbul airport, inaugurated in 2019, aims to handle between 150 and 200 million passengers a year by 2030, making it the world's largest airport, ahead of Atlanta. Turkey's ambition is accompanied by the rise of flag carrier Turkish Airlines, which operates both medium- and long-haul flights. Turkey's geographic position makes it an ideal hub not only between Asia and Europe but also between Asia and Africa: Istanbul is less than 4 h away by plane from London and Paris, 9 h from Beijing, 12 h from Tokyo, and 11 h from Cape Town. Turkey also boasts a large domestic market of more than 80 million inhabitants.

5.3.2.2 Toward a Hub War?

The rise of these new hubs has raised an initial question: to what extent will these new hubs impact traffic at existing hubs? These new hubs could pose a triple threat to airports such as Paris Charles De Gaulle, London Heathrow, and Frankfurt:

- On intercontinental flights with connections, passengers can now choose between several hubs in Europe or the Middle East. For example, a customer flying from Tokyo to Abidjan, which is on the coast of Côte d'Ivoire in West Africa, can choose to stop over in Paris, London, Istanbul, or Dubai.
- Middle Eastern hubs may begin threatening the viability of direct long-haul flights from Europe, by reducing aircraft load factors. For example, if an airline such as Emirates offers flights between Europe and Dubai and then between Dubai and Bangkok, the profitability of a direct flight between Paris and Bangkok may decline.
- Airlines backed by these new hubs open direct routes between regional European cities and their Middle East hub. Emirates, for example, offers a route from Nice to Tokyo via Dubai: two long-haul flights are operated, reducing unit costs. This strategy may call into question the hub strategy of an airline like Air France, which consists of taking passengers from Nice to Paris (on a short-haul flight) and then transferring them to a long-haul flight to Tokyo.

However, it's still too early to predict a real "hub war." An initial empirical study by Grosche and Klophaus (2015), based on data from 2012, concluded that the impact of these new hubs on Europe's major airports was fairly limited: the latter remained primarily in competition with each other to attract intercontinental and connecting flights from Europe. For example, Paris Charles de Gaulle airport's first four competitors were other European hubs: Frankfurt, Amsterdam, Munich, and London. However, at the time, Istanbul airport was already in sixth place, and Dubai and Doha in seventh and ninth places, respectively. The situation has changed since then: in a later study based on 2015 data, Grosche et al. (2017) found that the degree of competition between Middle Eastern and European hubs had increased, particularly with the strong rise of Istanbul: the latter has become the fourth competitor, in terms of number of competing connections, to airports such as Paris Charles de Gaulle, Amsterdam, and Brussels. Consequently, the largest threat to European hubs comes from Istanbul, which has become the largest airport in Europe in terms of number of air passengers.

Figure 5.3 shows the strong growth in the number of connections from hubs such as Doha (DOH), Dubai (DXB), and Istanbul (IST) over the 2009–2015 period, while the number of connections from Paris Charles de Gaulle (CDG), Frankfurt (FRA), and London Heathrow (LHR) stagnated or even declined over the same period.

Faced with this new competition from Middle Eastern and Turkish hubs and airlines, European airlines are trying to organize themselves and react by forging international code-share alliances with other airlines to secure their connecting traffic. For example, the alliance concluded in 2017 among US carrier Delta, Air France KLM, and Indian carrier Jet Airways (which has since been liquidated by the Supreme

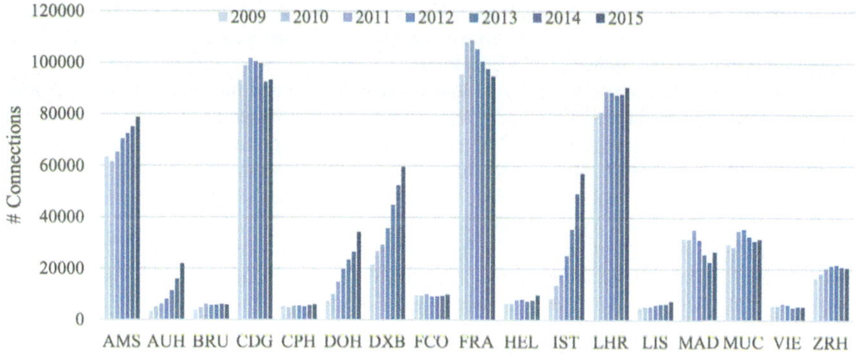

Fig. 5.3 Number of flight connections per hub (2009–2015). Source: Grosche et al. (2017)

Court of India) aimed to channel connecting traffic between the United States and India through Europe. The Gulf carriers, however, have adopted a similar alliance strategy: Quantas, for example, now connects via Dubai rather than Singapore.

A second question, more fundamental but delicate to address, is the extent to which these new airlines, whose prices are often highly competitive, are competing fairly with traditional American and European airlines. For example, according to Tretheway and Andriulaitis (2015) and De Wit (2015), the location of the Gulf carriers and Turkish Airlines in countries halfway between Asia, Europe, Africa, and the United States is a natural geographic advantage. Similarly, when comparing production costs, we need to take into account the size of the airlines and their average flight distance: for example, part of the cost advantage enjoyed by some Gulf airlines comes from their long-distance operations—on average, 4800 km for Emirates versus 2000 km for a company like Lufthansa.

There are also differences in national policies, in terms of, for example, airport taxes and oil prices. Insofar as foreign airlines are not discriminated against when operating from these countries, it is difficult to accuse them of "unfair competition" per se. In reality, the debate on unfair airline competition is primarily a question of whether or not governments give priority to air transport: some pundits now consider that, over and above its economic benefits, air transport is a vector of "soft power," while countries adopting a more or less proactive policy toward this sector.

References

Airbus. (2024). *Global Market Forecast 2023–2042*.

Chiambaretto, P., Mayenc, E., Chappert, H., Engsig, J., Fernandez, A.-S., & Le Roy, F. (2021). Where does flygskam come from? The role of citizens' lack of knowledge of the environmental impact of air transport in explaining the development of flight shame. *Journal of Air Transport Management, 93*, 102049.

Chiambaretto, P., Bildstein, C., Laurent, S., Rouyre, A., Chappert, C., Bovis, M., Levya-de la Hiz, D., Fernandez, A.-S., & Heritier, A. (2023). Towards a more sustainable aviation: The challenge of passengers acceptability. *Les Carnets de la Chaire Pégase*, n°5.

Chiambaretto, P., Laurent, S., Schmalz, U., Fu, M., Rouyre, A., Bildstein, C., & Fernandez, A.-S. (2024). Are consumers willing to pay more for green innovations? Insights from the air transport industry. *Technovation, 137*, 103079.

Dällenbach, N. (2020). Low-carbon travel mode choices: The role of time perceptions and familiarity. *Transportation Research Part D: Transport and Environment, 86*, 102378.

De Wit, J. (2015). *Unlevel playing field? Ah yes, you mean protectionism, 41*, 22–29.

Denstadli J. M., Gripsrud M., Hjorthol R., Julsrud,T. E. (2013) "Videoconferencing and business air travel: Do new technologies produce new interaction patterns?" *Transportation Research Part C: Emerging Technologies*, 29, pp. 1-13.

DGAC. (2019). *Calculateur d'émissions de gaz à effet de serre de l'aviation.*

Dobruszkes, F., Chen, C.-L., Moyano, A., Pagliara, F., & Endemann, P. (2022). Is high-speed rail socially exclusive? An evidence-based worldwide analysis. *Travel Behaviour and Society, 26*, 96–107.

EASA. (2024). *State of the EU SAF market in 2023*. Report, 88 p.

Fichert, F., & Klophaus, R. (2016). Self-connecting, codesharing and hubbing among European LCCs: From point-to-point to connections? *Research in Transportation Business & Management, 21*, 94–98.

Gössling, S., & Dolnicar, S. (2022). A review of air travel behavior and climate change. *Wiley Interdisciplinary Reviews: Climate Change, 14*, e802.

Gössling, S., Hanna, P., Higham, J., Cohen, S., & Hopkins, D. (2019). Can we fly less? Evaluating the 'necessity' of air travel. *Journal of Air Transport Management, 81*, 101722.

Grosche, T., & Klophaus, R. (2015). Hubs at risk: Exposure of Europe's largest hubs to competition on transfer city Pairs. *Transport Policy, 43*, 55–60.

Grosche, T., Klophaus, R., & Seredyński, A. (2017). Competition for long-haul connecting traffic among airports in Europe and the Middle East. *Journal of Air Transport Management, 64*, 3–14.

ICAO. (2022). *Guidance on potential policies and coordinated approaches for the deployment of sustainable aviation fuels.*

IEA. (2009). *Transport, Energy and CO2 – Moving toward Sustainability*. OECD.

Kollmuss, A., & Agyeman, J. (2002). Mind the gap: Why do people act environmentally and what are the barriers to pro-environmental behavior? *Environmental Education Research, 8*(3), 239–260.

Lee, D. S., Fahey, D. W., Skowron, A., Allen, M. R., Burkhardt, U., Chen, Q., et al. (2021). The contribution of global aviation to anthropogenic climate forcing for 2000 to 2018. *Atmospheric Environment, 244*, 117834.

Mkono, M. (2020). Eco-anxiety and the flight shaming movement: Implications for tourism. *Journal of Tourism Futures, 6*(3), 223–226.

Müller, A., & Wittmer, A. (2023). The choice between business travel and video conferencing after COVID-19 – Insights from a choice experiment among frequent travelers. *Tourism Management, 96*, 104688.

Rodrigue, J. P. (2020). *The geography of transport systems* (5th ed.). Routledge.

Roland Berger. (2022). *Future of long distance mobility: Study extract.*

Schäfer, A. W., Barrett, S. R. H., Doyme, K., Dray, L. M., Gnadt, A. R., Self, R., O'Sullivan, A., Synodinos, A. P., & Torija, A. J. (2019). Technological, economic and environmental prospects of all-electric aircraft. *Nature Energy, 4*(2), 160–166.

Scheelhaase, J., Maertens, S., Grimme, W., & Jung, M. (2018). EU ETS versus CORSIA – A critical assessment of two approaches to limit air transport's CO2 emissions by market-based measures. *Journal of Air Transport Management, 67*, 55–62.

Schmidt, F., Sidders, A., Czepkiewicz, M., Árnadóttir, Á., & Heinonen, J. (2024). 'I am not a typical flyer': Narratives about the justified or excessive character of international flights in a highly mobile society. *Journal of Sustainable Tourism, 32*(6), 1217–1240.

Spreen, W. (2019). *The aerospace business: Management and technology*. Routledge.

Tretheway, M., & Andriulaitis, R. (2015). What do we mean by a level playing field in international aviation? *Transport Policy, 43*, 96–103.

Conclusion

One hundred twenty years after the Wright brothers' first flight, air transport has found its raison d'être in the many services it provides every day to passengers all over the world: moving quickly and sometimes very far, whether for business or for pleasure, to visit family, study, seek medical care, and so on. Today, however, air transport is facing a double challenge: that of its profitability and that of its social legitimacy.

In terms of profitability, the opening up to competition and the emergence of a new business, low-cost model have made airlines the least profitable players in the sector's value chain. The challenge for the future is for airlines, and in particular the incumbents, to regain their leadership, whether by cutting costs, moving upmarket, or differentiating themselves. This task will be difficult to achieve because new entrants—especially those from the Middle East—have changed the landscape, particularly on long-haul routes.

From a societal standpoint, with more than 5 billion passengers expected in 2025 and an annual growth rate of 4% (IATA, 2024), the environmental impact of air transport is an important issue. Even if it accounts for only 3.5% of global greenhouse gas emissions, air transport should commit to a stronger decarbonization trajectory, without delay. As we have shown, these levers are regulatory and fiscal, as well as technological. The challenge is nothing short of inventing the aircraft of tomorrow.

P. Chiambaretto, E. Combe, *Introduction to Air Transport*, SpringerBriefs in Business, https://doi.org/10.1007/978-3-031-99936-9

References

ACI. (2015). *The impact of an airport.*
Airbus. (2024). *Global Market Forecast 2024-2043.*
Baker, D., Merkert, R., & Kamruzzaman, M. (2015). Regional aviation and economic growth: cointegration and causality analysis in Australia. *Journal of Transport Geography, 43*, 140–150.
Bel, G., & Fageda, X. (2008). Getting there fast: Globalization, intercontinental flights and location of headquarters. *Journal of Economic Geography, 8*(4), 471–495.
Blonigen, B., & Cristea, A. (2015). Air service and urban growth: Evidence from a quasi-natural policy experiment. *Journal of Urban Economics, 86*, 128–146.
Bråthen, S., & Halpern, N. (2012). Air transport service provision and management strategies to improve the economic benefits for remote regions. *Research in Transportation Business & Management, 4*, 3–12.
Bréchemier, D., & Combe, E. (2020). *After Covid-19, air transportation in Europe: The time for decision making*. Fondapol.
Chiambaretto, P., Bildstein, C., Alessandra, P., Rouyre, A., Feiereisen, S., Fernandez, A.-S., Seran, T., & Chappert, H. (2022). La génération Z et le transport aérien: quelles différences entre les 15-24 ans et le reste de la population française? *Les Carnets de la Chaire Pégase*, n°4.
Chiambaretto, P., Bildstein, C., Fernandez, A.-S., Alessandra, P., Chappert, H., Grall, M., Benmouri, M., Seran, T., Khedhaouria, A., & Papaix, C. (2021a). Voyages d'affaires et visioconférence : quel avenir pour le transport aérien?. *Les Carnets de la Chaire Pégase*, n°3.
Chiambaretto, P., Mayenc, E., Chappert, H., Engsig, J., Fernandez, A.-S., & Le Roy, F. (2021b). Where does flygskam come from? The role of citizens' lack of knowledge of the environmental impact of air transport in explaining the development of flight shame. *Journal of Air Transport Management, 93*, 102049.
Chiambaretto, P., Bildstein, C., Laurent, S., Rouyre, A., Chappert, C., Bovis, M., Levya-de la Hiz, D., Fernandez, A.-S., & Heritier, A. (2023). Towards a more sustainable aviation: The challenge of passengers acceptability. *Les Carnets de la Chaire Pégase*, n°5.
Chiambaretto, P., & Combe, E. (2023). Business model hybridization but heterogeneous economic performance: Insights from low-cost and legacy carriers in Europe. *Transport Policy, 136*, 83–97.
Chiambaretto, P., Laurent, S., Schmalz, U., Fu, M., Rouyre, A., Bildstein, C., & Fernandez, A.-S. (2024). Are consumers willing to pay more for green innovations? Insights from the air transport industry. *Technovation, 137*, 103079.
Combe, E. (2016). *La politique de la concurrence*. La Découverte, collection Repères (3rd ed.).
Combe, E. (2019). *Le low cost*. La Découverte, collection Repères (2nd ed.).

P. Chiambaretto, E. Combe, *Introduction to Air Transport*, SpringerBriefs in Business, https://doi.org/10.1007/978-3-031-99936-9

Combe, E. (2021). *Competition policy: An empirical and economic approach*. Wolters Kluwer.
Dällenbach, N. (2020). Low-carbon travel mode choices: The role of time perceptions and familiarity. *Transportation Research Part D: Transport and Environment, 86*, 102378.
De Wit, J. (2015). *Unlevel playing field? Ah yes, you mean protectionism, 41*, 22–29.
Denstadli J. M., Gripsrud M., Hjorthol R., Julsrud,T. E. (2013) "Videoconferencing and business air travel: Do new technologies produce new interaction patterns?" *Transportation Research Part C: Emerging Technologies*, 29, pp. 1-13.
DGAC. (2007). La demande de transport aérien: Comment l'expliquer ? Peut-on la prévoir? *Les notes thématiques*, n° 5, 4 p.
DGAC. (2019). *Calculateur d'émissions de gaz à effet de serre de l'aviation.*
Dobruszkes, F., Chen, C.-L., Moyano, A., Pagliara, F., & Endemann, P. (2022). Is high-speed rail socially exclusive? An evidence-based worldwide analysis. *Travel Behaviour and Society, 26*, 96–107.
EASA. (2024). *State of the EU SAF market il 2023*. Report, 88 p.
Ennen, D., Allroggen, F., & Malina, R. (2019). *On-stop versus connecting air services: Airfares, costs and consumers' willingness to pay*. Massachusetts Institute of Technology, Report No. ICAT-2019-03, MIT International Center for Air Transportation (ICAT).
Fichert, F., & Klophaus, R. (2016). Self-connecting, codesharing and hubbing among European LCCs: From point-to-point to connections? *Research in Transportation Business & Management, 21*, 94–98.
Gillen, D., Morrison, W., & Stewart, C. (2008). *Air travel demand elasticities: Concepts, issues and measurement*. Government of Canada, Department of Finance.
Gössling, S., & Dolnicar, S. (2022). A review of air travel behavior and climate change. *Wiley Interdisciplinary Reviews: Climate Change, 14*, e802.
Gössling, S., Hanna, P., Higham, J., Cohen, S., & Hopkins, D. (2019). Can we fly less? Evaluating the 'necessity' of air travel. *Journal of Air Transport Management, 81*, 101722.
Grammich, C., & DaVanzo, J. (2008). *Enhancing small-business opportunities in the DoD*. Technical report, 128 p.
Green, R. (2007). Airports and economic development. *Real Estate Economics, 35*(1), 91–112.
Grosche, T., & Klophaus, R. (2015). Hubs at risk: Exposure of Europe's largest hubs to competition on transfer city Pairs. *Transport Policy, 43*, 55–60.
Grosche, T., Klophaus, R., & Seredyński, A. (2017). Competition for long-haul connecting traffic among airports in Europe and the Middle East. *Journal of Air Transport Management, 64*, 3–14.
Hortelano, A. O., Guzman, A. F., Preston, J., & Vassallo, J. M. (2016). Price elasticity of demand on the high-speed rail lines of Spain: Impact of the new pricing scheme. *Transportation Research Record, 2597*(1), 90–98.
IATA. (2011). *Vision 2050.*
IATA. (2022). *Outsized market power in parts of the aviation value chain*. IATA Economics' Chart of the Week.
IATA. (2024). *Strengthened profitability expected in 2025 even as supply chain issues persist.*
ICAO. (2013). 50th Conference of Directors General of Civil Aviation Asia and Pacific Regions Economic development of air transport Current Challenges, 42 p.
ICAO. (2020). *Aviation benefits report.*
ICAO. (2022). *Guidance on potential policies and coordinated approaches for the deployment of sustainable aviation fuels.*
IEA. (2009). *Transport, Energy and CO2 – Moving toward Sustainability*. OECD.
Kollmuss, A., & Agyeman, J. (2002). Mind the gap: Why do people act environmentally and what are the barriers to pro-environmental behavior? *Environmental Education Research, 8*(3), 239–260.
Kuljanin, J., & Kalic, M. (2016). The uprise of the middle east carriers: Emirates' path towards success. *Symorg Conference*, 1405–1412.

Lee, D. S., Fahey, D. W., Skowron, A., Allen, M. R., Burkhardt, U., Chen, Q., et al. (2021). The contribution of global aviation to anthropogenic climate forcing for 2000 to 2018. *Atmospheric Environment, 244*, 117834.

Malighetti, P., Paleari, S., & Redondi, R. (2009). Pricing strategies of low-cost airlines: The Ryanair case study. *Journal of Air Transport Management, 15*(4), 195–203.

Mkono, M. (2020). Eco-anxiety and the flight shaming movement: Implications for tourism. *Journal of Tourism Futures, 6*(3), 223–226.

Morrison, J., Sgouridis, S., & Hansman, R. (2011). *Game theory analysis if aircraft manufacturer innovation strategies in the face of increasing airline fuel costs*. Report No. ICAT-2011-4, MIT International Center for Air Transportation.

Morrison, S. (2001). Actual, adjacent and potential competition: Estimating the full impact of Southwest Airlines. *Journal of Transport Economics and Policy, 35*, 239–256.

Mukkala, K., & Tervo, H. (2013). Air transportation and regional growth: Which way does the causality run? *Environment and Planning A, 45*(6), 1508–1520.

Müller, A., & Wittmer, A. (2023). The choice between business travel and video conferencing after COVID-19 – Insights from a choice experiment among frequent travelers. *Tourism Management, 96*, 104688.

Our World in Data. (2022). *Global aviation fatalities per million passengers*.

Pilot Career News. (2022). *Eurocontrol: rise of the low cost carriers*.

Porter, M. (1985). *Competitive advantage*. Dunod.

PwC. (2014). *Connectivity and growth: Directions of travel for airport investments*.

Rodrigue, J. P. (2020). *The geography of transport systems* (5th ed.). Routledge.

Roland Berger. (2022). *Future of long distance mobility: Study extract.*

Schäfer, A. W., Barrett, S. R. H., Doyme, K., Dray, L. M., Gnadt, A. R., Self, R., O'Sullivan, A., Synodinos, A. P., & Torija, A. J. (2019). Technological, economic and environmental prospects of all-electric aircraft. *Nature Energy, 4*(2), 160–166.

Scheelhaase, J., Maertens, S., Grimme, W., & Jung, M. (2018). EU ETS versus CORSIA – A critical assessment of two approaches to limit air transport's CO2 emissions by market-based measures. *Journal of Air Transport Management, 67*, 55–62.

Schmidt, F., Sidders, A., Czepkiewicz, M., Árnadóttir, Á., & Heinonen, J. (2024). 'I am not a typical flyer': Narratives about the justified or excessive character of international flights in a highly mobile society. *Journal of Sustainable Tourism, 32*(6), 1217–1240.

Soyk, C., Ringbeck, P., & Spinler, S. (2017). Long-haul low cost airlines: Characteristics of the business model and sustainability of its cost advantages. *Transportation Research Part A Policy and Practice, 106*, 215–234.

Spreen, W. (2019). *The aerospace business: Management and technology*. Routledge.

Tirole, J. (1988). *The theory of industrial organization*. MIT Press.

Tittle, D., McCarthy, P., & Xiao, Y. (2012). Airport runway capacity and economic development: A panel data analysis of metropolitan statistical areas. *Economic Development Quarterly, 27*(3), 230–239.

Tretheway, M., & Andriulaitis, R. (2015). What do we mean by a level playing field in international aviation? *Transport Policy, 43*, 96–103.

Warnock-Smith, D., O'Connell, J., & Maleki, M. (2015). *An examination of ongoing trends in airline ancillary revenues*. The 19th Air Transport Research Society (ATRS) World Conference, Singapore.

Xia, W., & Zhang, A. (2016). High-speed rail and air transport competition and cooperation: A vertical differentiation approach. *Transportation Research Part B: Methodological, 94*, 456–481.

Zhang, F., & Graham, D. J. (2020). Air transport and economic growth: A review of the impact mechanism and causal relationships. *Transport Reviews, 40*(4), 506–528.

The manufacturer's authorised representative in the EU is Springer
Nature Customer Service Centre GmbH, Europaplatz 3, 69115 Heidelberg,
Germany. If you have any concerns regarding our products, please
contact ProductSafety@springernature.com

Printed and bound by CPI Group (UK) Ltd, Croydon, CR0 4YY
30/09/2026
02225575-0008